A COZY BOOK
OF BREAKFASTS
& BRUNCHES

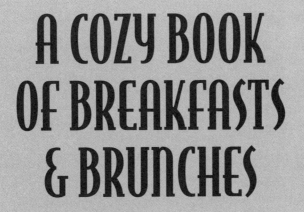

A COZY BOOK OF BREAKFASTS & BRUNCHES

Jim Brown
Karletta Moniz

PRIMA PUBLISHING

PRIMA PUBLISHING and its colophon are trademarks of Prima Communications, Inc.

Library of Congress Cataloging-in-Publication Data
Brown, James L.
    A cozy book of breakfasts & brunches / James L. Brown and Karletta Moniz.
        p.   cm.
    Includes index.
    ISBN 0-7615-0453-2
    1. Breakfasts.   2. Brunches.   I. Moniz, Karletta.   II. Title.
TX733.B72   1996
641.5'2—dc20   96-29193
                                                               CIP

97 98 99 AA 10 9 8 7 6 5 4 3 2 1
Printed in the United States of America

All products mentioned in this book are trademarks of their respective companies.

How to Order
Single copies may be ordered from Prima Publishing, P.O. Box 1260, Rocklin, CA 95677; telephone (916) 632-4400. Quantity discounts are also available. On your letterhead, include information concerning the intended use of the books and the number of books you wish to purchase. Visit us online at http://www.primapublishing.com

For Tom,
a real
breakfast enthusiast

Contents

Recipe Listing

Meat and Potatoes

Fruit for Breakfast

Breakfast Drinks and Beverages

Acknowledgements

Our thanks to those of you who encouraged and supported us throughout this project, especially Jim and Merilyn Brown, Evelyn Clark, Lurline Felts, Doug Garrett, Dennis Gray, Chris Meints, Jennife Basye Sander, Kelli Ann Walker, and Jane Bernath Whitehead.

INTRODUCTION

When did we all become so busy? All too often, mealtime seems like just another obligation to be worked into the schedule, another logistical challenge. For many people, the idea of starting the day by setting aside time to prepare and enjoy fresh, flavorful food is just so much wishful thinking. And isn't that the point?

In a world with so many demands and obligations, what could be more valuable than the small amount of time we set aside for ourselves? This is the reason for taking breakfast seriously.

For those of us who love breakfast, the appeal of the morning meal has as much to do with the process as with the product. Brewing coffee, pouring juice, stirring a gently bubbling pot of oatmeal, and buttering toast are their own rewards. These simple tasks make up the orderly ritual by which we ease into the new day. Our mothers and grandmothers were right—a good breakfast is the key to a productive day.

What We Eat in the Morning

For some of us, each morning really is a bright, new beginning. The rest of us rise and shine somewhat more reluctantly.

What we choose to eat first thing in the morning is just as personal. This may explain the singular pleasure of making a breakfast out of last night's cold pizza, preferably eaten straight from the refrigerator. (Actually, leftovers for breakfast is not a new idea. This is how the ancient Romans typically started their day.)

When we consider the traditional American breakfast foods, however, we find a meal that adheres to strict conventions. Eggs and dairy products predominate, with eggs consumed as a main dish (as opposed to being supporting ingredients for other foods) and milk enjoyed as a drink or used to moisten hot or cold cereals. Meat appears as an accompaniment—specifically, fried or broiled, not roasted or grilled—and seldom as a main dish. The meat is almost always pork (cured, not fresh), rarely poultry or fish, almost never beef.

Breakfast vegetables are limited primarily to potatoes. We eat mushrooms, onions, and peppers as ingredients in fillings or garnishes, and tomatoes as a garnish or juice. But we seldom eat greens, squash, or beans in the morning.

Breakfast food features a variety of flavors and textures, many with specific meanings. Sweetness and creaminess are common characteristics, as if only the promise of dessert can

"Only dull people are brilliant at breakfast."
    —Oscar Wilde

tempt us to face the day. Fresh fruit and simple grains and cereals supply the morning meal with an aura of humble, virtuous purity. Tart, cold juices and strong, hot coffee challenge and invigorate.

About Our Recipes

We wrote this book for readers who have basic experience in the kitchen, although we feel confidence, patience, and a sense of adventure are the most useful qualities for anyone who cooks. Breakfast food is, by nature, among the simplest and most straightforward food we prepare throughout the day. So are most of our recipes; the few that are more involved are not difficult to execute. Like most recipes, ours give specific instructions and measurements where it counts, but don't hesitate to experiment—this is how to make our favorite recipes your own.

A word about ingredients. Our society places such emphasis on personal gratification and freedom, yet we live in a time when food is suspect and one's own appetite is a force to be resisted. Healthfulness and indulgence are polar extremes at breakfast, and our recipes reflect the breadth of that spectrum. Satisfaction comes with balance, moderation, and common

"Cooking is just like religion. Rules don't no more make a cook than sermons make a saint."

–Anonymous

sense: indulge in rich breakfast favorites occasionally but not at the expense of the fresh, wholesome, flavorful treats we also offer. (And remember, for as much care and attention as cooking and eating deserve, we should never look to food alone as a panacea. Exercise, rest, laughter, and love are just as important for health and satisfaction.)

Our recipes call for butter because we value its unequaled flavor. We specifically prefer unsalted butter, because it is generally fresher than the salted variety (salt is a preservative) and it gives both cook and diner more control over flavors. Margarine is an acceptable substitute where butter isn't a central player; however, ingredients such as water, milk solids, and thickeners that help impart butter-like qualities often make margarine unsuitable for baking or frying (and not necessarily lower in calories or fat, either—read all labels carefully). The use of nonstick cookware simplifies cooking and cleanup and allows as little fat as necessary.

Eggs present a similar challenge. For those concerned about cholesterol, commercially available egg substitutes will work in some recipes, so long as the cook understands the differences and limitations presented by these products. Simpler substitutions, such as an egg white for a whole egg, often make a significant difference without affecting the chemical processes taking place in the preparation.

"Eatest thou always onions for breakfast?" Augustín asked.

"When there are any."

"Do all in thy country do this?"

"Nay," Robert Jordan said. "It is looked on badly there."

"I am glad," Augustín said. "I had always considered America a civilized country."

   —from *For Whom the Bell Tolls* by Ernest Hemingway

1

EGGS

Consider the egg: elegantly simple inside and out; the very symbol of birth and rebirth; inexpensive, easy to prepare, flavorful, and nutritious. Could there possibly be a more appropriate food with which to start the day? For many of us, breakfast means eggs.

Eggs As Healthful Food

The egg is a complex package. Half of its composition is water, a third is fat, and the rest is protein. The white contains most of the water and protein, while the yolk contains most of the vitamins and minerals, three-quarters of the calories, and most of the cholesterol.

Due to concerns about fat and cholesterol, many of us are eating eggs more selectively (despite recent studies that raise new questions about earlier warnings concerning the health risks of eating eggs). As a result, the market for commercial egg substitutes flourishes. Although seldom served by themselves, commercial egg substitutes can stand in where the egg is not the centerpiece. Many substitutes contain no cholesterol, but they're nearly as high in sodium as real eggs, so always read the label.

Alternatively, many egg recipes can be lightened without difficulty by replacing some of the eggs with one or more egg whites. For example, an egg white in place of one whole egg would go nearly unnoticed in a scramble, omelette, or frittata. But don't overdo it: the yolk contributes considerable moisture, which egg whites cannot supply.

Eggs for a Quick and Easy Breakfast

For the most part, eggs are among the easiest breakfast foods to prepare. Even more complex preparations, such as poached eggs or omelettes, require only a little practice.

"Eggs of an hour, bread of a day, wine of a year, a friend of thirty years."

–an Italian saying

Fried Eggs: The Technique

We prefer eating fried eggs with a dash of hot sauce and a fresh grinding of black pepper. They're equally delicious with crisp bacon or sausage or served over-easy atop Chicken Hash (page 87).

SERVES 1

1 tablespoon unsalted butter
1 egg, broken into a small dish

In an 8-inch nonstick skillet, melt the butter over medium heat until a drop of water sizzles when dropped into the pan. Carefully drop the egg into the pan and lower the heat. For sunny-side up, cook the egg on one side only until the white is set and the yolk is soft—do not turn it over. For over-easy, cook the egg sunny-side up, but turn it over before the white sets completely. Cook the second side until the white sets but the yolk is still soft. For over-medium, cook an egg over-easy and continue to cook until the yolk is almost set.

Huevos Rancheros O'Neal

The following recipe comes from a family friend in San Antonio, Texas. It's completely authentic in its simplicity, and it's delicious, too!

SERVES 1

1 small tomato
1 tablespoon chopped, seeded jalapeño pepper
2 tablespoons chopped onion
pinch dried oregano
salt and black pepper to taste
3 tablespoons unsalted butter
1 corn tortilla
2 eggs

Preheat the oven to 200 degrees F. In a blender, place the tomato, jalapeño and onion. Blend until smooth, adding a few drops of water if the mixture seems dry. Place the sauce in a small saucepan and heat over medium heat. Season with the oregano, salt, and pepper. Cover the pan and set aside to keep warm.

In a 10- to 12-inch nonstick skillet, melt 1 tablespoon of the butter over medium heat. Place the tortilla in the skillet and heat briefly until warm. Remove the tortilla from the pan, wrap it in foil, and place it in the oven to keep warm. In the same pan, add the remaining 2 tablespoons of butter and fry the eggs as preferred.

To serve, place the eggs on the tortilla and cover with the sauce. Serve immediately.

"At a formal breakfast, all precautions should be taken to insure the freshness of the eggs. A conscientious hostess would be very much mortified if she served chicken out of its proper course."
    –Olive Green, *What to Have for Breakfast* (1905)

Poached Eggs: The Technique

Poached eggs are simply eggs simmered briefly without the shell. A correctly poached egg is moist and soft, not hard-boiled. The technique takes practice but makes an impressive addition to one's breakfast repertoire.

SERVES 1

1 egg
4 tablespoons white vinegar

To a large skillet that can hold at least three inches of water, add 4 tablespoons of white vinegar for every quart of water used (the vinegar helps the eggs whites to firm up). Bring the water to a full boil.

Break an egg into a custard cup. With a spoon, swirl the water in the skillet to form a whirlpool. Holding the cup just above the water, gently drop the egg into the center of the whirlpool. The movement of the water helps the white surround the yolk evenly. Reduce the heat to a simmer and cook for three minutes.

Using a slotted spoon, carefully lift the egg onto a paper towel and blot it dry. Trim way any uneven edges to make a nicely rounded shape, and serve.

If you're making poached eggs for a crowd, keep them in a bowl of cold water in the refrigerator until ready to serve.

Reheat by lowering each egg into a pan of hot water for one minute.

Eggs Benedict

In this age of healthy, low-fat eating, this recipe does seem a bit decadent. However, everyone deserves to enjoy this delicious classic at least occasionally. Try it for a special occasion, like Mother's Day. Be sure to reserve your egg whites for making Ramos Gin Fizzes (see page 116).

SERVES 4

1 tablespoon butter
8 slices Canadian bacon
4 English muffins, toasted lightly
8 poached eggs
1 cup Hollandaise sauce (recipe follows)
8 black olives, pitted

Preheat the oven to 200 degrees F. In a 10- to 12-inch nonstick skillet, melt the butter over medium heat. Add the Canadian bacon, laying the slices flat, and cook for 2 to 3 minutes, or until warm. Remove the slices from the skillet, wrap in aluminum foil, and place in the oven to keep warm.

Assemble each serving by placing two muffin halves on each plate. Top each half with one slice of Canadian bacon, one poached egg, approximately 2 tablespoons of Hollandaise sauce, and 1 olive. Serve immediately.

Eggs Benedict is said to have been created at Manhattan's famous Delmonico's restaurant where a certain Mr. and Mrs. LeGrand Benedict, regular patrons, complained that there was nothing new on the lunch menu.

Hollandaise Sauce

Makes 1 cup

12 tablespoons (1 1/2 sticks) plus 1 tablespoon chilled
    unsalted butter
3 egg yolks
1 tablespoon lemon juice
1 tablespoon heavy cream
salt and white pepper to taste

Melt the 12 tablespoons of butter in a small saucepan over low
heat or in a small glass bowl in the microwave. Let the golden
butterfat separate from the whitish milk solids, then slowly
pour just the oil into a small pitcher or measuring cup with a
pouring spout. Set the pitcher or cup in a small bowl half-filled
with warm water to keep warm.

    Place several inches of water in a 2-quart saucepan, bring
it to a boil, then reduce to a simmer. On top of the pan set a
nonreactive bowl large enough so that the pan does not touch
the water below. Place the egg yolks in the bowl and whisk
constantly until they become quite thick (this will take several
minutes—do not turn up the heat to hurry the process).
Add the lemon juice and beat until completely incorporated.
Whisk in the 1 tablespoon of chilled butter. Continue whisking until the mixture is thick enough to lightly coat the back
of a spoon, but avoid allowing the mixture to curdle like

scrambled eggs. Remove the bowl from the heat and whisk in the cream.

Set the bowl on a flat surface on top of a coiled-up kitchen towel for stability (or have someone hold the bowl for you) and begin adding the melted butter drop by drop, whisking constantly with the other hand. The mixture will slowly thicken as you continue whisking in the butter. When all the butter has been added, taste the sauce and season it with the salt and pepper. Serve immediately.

Scrambled Eggs: The Technique

Properly cooked, scrambled eggs should be moist and creamy, not rubbery, grainy, or dry. The addition of a small amount of liquid helps the yolk to blend with the white and thicken smoothly.

The best scrambled eggs we've ever had were prepared for us by an experienced cook, who simply added a pinch of dried fines herbes to the egg mixture before cooking.

SERVES 1

2 eggs
1 tablespoon whole or low-fat milk
pinch each salt and black pepper
1 to 2 tablespoons unsalted butter

Beat the eggs, milk, salt, and pepper until well blended. Melt the butter over medium-high heat in an 8-inch nonstick skillet. Pour the eggs in the skillet. Reduce the heat to low and cook,

The color of an egg's shell reflects the hen's breed and is unrelated to its nutritive value. The shells of brown eggs are thicker than those of white eggs, which makes them more resistant to cracking when boiled.

15

stirring slowly, until the eggs begin to firm up. Lift the sides of the eggs along the edge of the pan to allow the uncooked portion to run underneath. The eggs are ready when they are just set and still soft, with a nice shine to them. Remove from the heat and serve immediately.

Ham Scramble

SERVES 1

1 tablespoon unsalted butter
1 tablespoon chopped onion
1/4 cup diced cooked ham
Scrambled Eggs (see above)

Melt the butter in an 8-inch nonstick skillet over medium heat. Add the onion and cook until translucent. Add the ham and cook only until heated through. In a second 8-inch nonstick skillet, prepare the scrambled eggs as described above. Just before the eggs have set completely, stir in the onion and ham mixture. Continue cooking until the eggs set, then serve.

Joe's Special

This savory scramble was supposedly invented at Original Joe's in San Francisco as a late-night whim with the only ingredients at hand. It's been served daily there since the late 1930s. We like to imagine Sam Spade showing up to enjoy this specialty as a late-night breakfast.

Karletta's mother captivated dinner parties in the early 1960s with this particular version of the classic recipe. Leftovers are wonderful eaten cold as a sandwich filling between two slices of sourdough bread and plenty of mayonnaise.

SERVES 4 TO 6

2 tablespoons olive oil
2 pounds lean ground beef
1 large onion, chopped
2 teaspoons minced garlic
3/4 pound mushrooms, thinly sliced
1 teaspoon salt
1 teaspoon freshly ground black pepper
1 teaspoon chopped fresh oregano
1/2 pound fresh spinach, washed thoroughly, drained,
    and chopped
6 eggs

In a 10- to 12-inch nonstick skillet, heat the oil over medium-high heat and brown the ground beef. Add onion, garlic, and mushrooms and cook until the onion is translucent. Add salt, pepper, and oregano. Stir well. Spread the chopped spinach across the meat mixture, cover the pan, and allow the spinach to wilt for approximately 5 minutes. Meanwhile, beat the eggs and 1 tablespoon of water in a small mixing bowl. When the spinach is ready, pour in the eggs and stir gently until the eggs have set completely. Serve warm.

Herb Scramble

SERVES 1

Scrambled Eggs (see above)
1 teaspoon finely chopped Italian (flat-leaf) parsley or chives,
    or 1/2 teaspoon dried fines herbes

Prepare the scrambled eggs as described above. Sprinkle the herbs just before the eggs have set completely. Continue cooking until the eggs set, then serve.

Omelettes: The Technique

Despite their French pedigree, omelettes are quite easy to master. If you're at all intimidated, we suggest you spend a Saturday morning with a dozen eggs, a good omelette pan, and a few good friends to cheer you on. At worst, you'll just end up with scrambled eggs!

SERVES 1

3 eggs
pinch each salt and black pepper
3 tablespoons unsalted butter

Break the eggs into a medium stainless steel or glass bowl and add 2 teaspoons water, salt, and pepper. Beat well with a wire whisk until well blended. In an 8-inch nonstick omelette pan (or heavy skillet with a flat bottom), melt the butter over medium-high heat until it just begins to brown (watch it closely). Pour the egg mixture into the pan.

Immediately the eggs will turn opaque along the edges. As the bottom of the omelette begins to set, slip a small spatula around the edge and let the uncooked egg ooze over the edge and under the omelette. Continue until the egg on top is no longer runny and the top still looks shiny.

If the omelette is to be filled, place the filling on the left half of the omelette, about one inch from the center and from the outer edges. Fold the right half over the left half. Shake the pan to loosen the omelette. Carefully slide the omelette onto a warm serving plate.

Omelette with Smoked Ham and Gruyère

The flavors of this omelette remind us of a classic French quiche.

SERVES 1

Omelette (see above)
1/4 cup shredded Gruyère or Swiss cheese
2 slices of thinly sliced smoked ham (about 1 ounce each)
1 teaspoon chopped chives

Prepare the omelette as described above. Before folding, place the cheese and ham along the center of the omelette. Fold the omelette and top with chives.

"An egg is always an adventure; the next one may be different."

–Oscar Wilde

19

Omelette with Green Chilies, Avocado, and Monterey Jack Cheese

Serve with warm flour or corn tortillas.

SERVES 1

Omelette (see above)
2 tablespoons diced canned green chilies
1/4 cup mashed ripe avocado
1/4 cup shredded Monterey Jack cheese
2 tablespoons sour cream

Prepare the omelette as described above. Before folding, place the chilies, avocado, and cheese along the center of the omelette. Fold the omelette and top with sour cream.

Bacon and Spinach Omelette

This variation is delicious served with lightly buttered rye toast.

SERVES 1

Omelette (see above)
1/2 cup cooked spinach, squeezed dry and chopped coarsely
2 strips of crisply cooked bacon, crumbled
1/4 cup shredded Monterey Jack cheese
3 slices ripe tomato

Prepare the omelette as described above. Before folding, spread the spinach along the center of the omelette. Top the spinach with bacon and cheese. Fold the omelette, transfer to a serving plate, and garnish with tomato slices.

Chile Relleno Casserole

This is a great brunch dish. Although you cannot prepare this one the night before, the actual assembly is easily done once all of your guests have arrived. Warmed flour or corn tortillas make a nice accompaniment.

SERVES 8

12 eggs, separated
2 tablespoons all-purpose bleached flour
$^1/_2$ teaspoon salt
$^1/_2$ teaspoon garlic powder
$^1/_2$ teaspoon black pepper, freshly ground
7 ounces canned green chilies, rinsed, seeded, and patted dry
$^1/_2$ pound cheddar cheese, grated
$^1/_2$ teaspoon paprika
1 cup salsa
1 cup sour cream

Preheat the oven to 350 degrees F. In a large mixing bowl, beat the egg whites until stiff. Set aside. In a separate mixing bowl, beat the egg yolks, flour, salt, garlic powder, and pepper until frothy. Carefully fold the whites into the egg yolk mixture. Pour half of this mixture into a buttered 9 × 13-inch baking dish. Layer the chilies and cheese over the eggs. Cover with the remaining egg mixture. Sprinkle with paprika. Bake for 30 minutes or until the eggs have completely set and the top is lightly browned. Serve warm, topped with salsa and sour cream.

21

Frittata

This is an Italian relative of the omelette, although Italians will quickly tell you the two must not be confused. Unlike the omelette, a frittata is cooked slowly over lower heat, it's drier and firmer, it's flipped over and cooked on both sides, and it's round and flat.

Most important, it's easily adapted to fillings and flavorings that are on hand. We find it the perfect solution whenever we get carried away buying produce at the local farmers' market. Add a few stalks of chopped, blanched asparagus to the skillet right before pouring in the egg mixture—delicious! Or just before placing the frittata in the oven, how about slicing a couple of those beautiful tomatoes over the top and sprinkling them with minced fresh oregano? Inspired!

SERVES 4 TO 6

2 tablespoons olive oil
1/3 cup chopped onion
2 tablespoons chopped fresh basil
1/4 cup grated Parmesan cheese
salt and black pepper to taste
7 large eggs, beaten

Preheat the oven to 350 degrees F. In a 12-inch ovenproof, nonstick skillet, heat the olive oil over medium-high heat and quickly sauté the onion until translucent. While the onions are cooking, mix the basil, cheese, salt, pepper, and eggs in a small bowl. Pour the mixture over the onions, stirring with a fork until the eggs begin to cook, then stop stirring. As the mixture begins to set, gently lift the edge with a spatula, allowing the uncooked egg from the top to flow under. Let the eggs set further, then repeat lifting the edge with the spatula until there is no longer any uncooked egg on top.

Place the skillet in the oven on the top rack. Bake until the frittata is dry, 3 to 5 minutes. Do not overcook the frittata, or it will have a rubbery texture. Remove from the oven. With a sharp paring knife, carefully loosen the frittata around the edges and ease onto a serving plate. Serve warm or at room temperature.

To neatly separate an egg, place a small funnel in a cup. Gently break the egg into the funnel. The white will run out the bottom into the cup, leaving the yolk behind.

Hangtown Fry

This rich and unusual dish—essentially an oyster frittata—dates from the Gold Rush. It is named for Hangtown, the brawling Mother Lode town now called Placerville, which is located northeast of San Francisco and just over the hill from Sutter's Mill, where gold was first discovered in California. Some say the dish was created for a newly rich miner who ordered dinner made with the restaurant's most expensive ingredients. Others say it was the last supper requested by an outlaw doomed to hang. Helen Brown, author of the venerable West Coast Cookbook, offers the most plausible, if somewhat less romantic, explanation: a Hangtown bartender created the dish during the Gold Rush days and popularized it at a restaurant he later opened in San Francisco.

SERVES 4

1/4 pound sliced bacon
1/2 cup all-purpose flour
7 eggs
1/2 cup dry sourdough breadcrumbs
4 to 6 medium raw oysters, shucked and patted dry
4 tablespoons (1/4 cup) unsalted butter
salt and black pepper to taste
4 slices sourdough bread, toasted

Preheat the oven to 350 degrees F. In a 10- to 12-inch oven-proof, nonstick skillet, fry the bacon over low heat until crisp. Remove the bacon to drain on paper towels and keep it warm by covering with foil.

Line up three shallow dishes and place the flour in the first dish, one egg (beaten) in the second dish, and the bread-crumbs in the third dish. Roll each oyster in the flour, shaking off any excess, then dip it in the egg and finally in the breadcrumbs. Lightly pat on the crumbs to coat each oyster completely.

Carefully pour the bacon grease from the skillet into a heat-proof container and set aside to cool completely before discarding. Add the butter and melt over medium heat. Place all of the oysters in the heated skillet and brown on each side. (Be sure the pan is hot enough. It is ready when the oysters quietly sizzle when they're added—otherwise, turn up the heat slightly.) While the oysters are cooking, beat the remaining six eggs, salt, and pepper in a medium bowl. Once the oysters are browned on both sides, pour in the egg mixture. As the egg mixture begins to set, gently lift the edge with a spatula and let the uncooked egg from the top run underneath. Repeat lifting the edge with the spatula until there is no more runny egg on top.

Lay the bacon strips on top of the eggs and place the skillet in the oven on the top rack. Bake until dry, 3 to 5 minutes. With a sharp paring knife, carefully loosen the eggs around the edges and ease onto a warm serving plate. Serve warm with sourdough toast.

Union Square Brunch

We enjoy having family over for Christmas Eve brunch. Afterwards, we walk down the hill to Union Square, San Francisco's central shopping district, to admire the decorated storefronts and perhaps indulge in some last-minute shopping. We wanted a dish we could prepare the night before and just pop in the oven. This is it. Essentially a savory bread pudding, it makes an entire meal when served with a tossed green salad and champagne.

SERVES 4 TO 6

8 tablespoons (1 stick) unsalted butter
1/2 pound mushrooms, thinly sliced
2 cups onion, thinly sliced
1 tablespoon vegetable oil
1 1/2 pounds Sweet Italian Chicken Sausage (page 81)
    or any mild Italian turkey sausage, casings removed
12 slices of good-quality white bread, crusts removed
3/4 pound sharp cheddar cheese, coarsely grated
6 eggs, beaten
2 1/2 cups whole or low-fat milk
1 teaspoon dry mustard
1 tablespoon Dijon-style prepared mustard
1 teaspoon nutmeg (preferably freshly ground)
2 tablespoons finely chopped, fresh Italian parsley

In a 10- to 12-inch nonstick skillet, melt the butter over medium-high heat. Add the mushrooms and onion, cooking until the onions are translucent. Remove from the pan to a medium heat-proof bowl and set aside. In the same skillet, heat the oil and brown the sausage. Drain well and add to the mushroom-onion mixture.

Butter a 9 × 13-inch ovenproof baking dish and cover the bottom with half of the bread, then half of the mushroom-onion-sausage mixture, then half of the cheese. Make another layer with the remaining bread, mushroom-onion-sausage mixture, and cheese. In a medium mixing bowl, mix the cheese, eggs, milk, both mustards, and nutmeg. Pour this mixture over the layers in the baking dish. Cover and refrigerate overnight.

The next day, preheat the oven to 350 degrees F. Remove the baking dish from the refrigerator, uncover it, and sprinkle the parsley over the top. Bake, uncovered, for one hour, until the top is brown and the eggs are set completely.

2

CEREALS
HOT AND COLD

Inexpensive to purchase, easy to store, and simple to prepare, cereals and grains lend the morning meal a sense of humble, healthful purity.

Cereals and grains offer us much at breakfast-time. They are healthful and easy to prepare. Cooked cereals warm and soothe us—the mealtime equivalent to snuggling back under the covers to catch a few more minutes of sleep. In contrast, the satisfying crunch of cold cereal seems to stimulate and enliven us, as if wakefulness and health are accomplished with plenty of noisy effort.

Hot Cereals for Cold Mornings

The most familiar of all hot cereals is oatmeal. A native of Scotland, where the climate is inhospitable to wheat, this cereal in its unprocessed form is normally used as animal fodder. Despite a humble image, however, oats are also among the most nutritious cereals.

The uncooked cereal comes in two forms. Rolled oats are hulled oat berries (sometimes called oat groats) that have been steam-heated and flattened between heavy rollers. Steel-cut oats, also called Scotch or Irish oats, are hulled oat berries

Samuel Johnson, in his 1755 *Dictionary of the English Language*, defined "oats" as "a grain which in England is generally given to horses, but which in Scotland supports the people."

cut into a coarse meal. Either method of processing keeps the cooking time to a minimum.

Other hot breakfast cereals include cream of wheat and cream of rice, both of which are meals made from processed cereal. Less familiar cereals worth trying for breakfast include cracked wheat, which is made from the whole wheat berry; bulgur wheat, which is a Middle Eastern staple made from wheat berries that have been steamed, dried, and crushed (the latter makes a more substantial hot cereal, while the former is lighter); and buckwheat groats, which is the hulled, crushed kernel of the plant sometimes called "poor man's wheat" (toasted buckwheat groats are known as kasha).

Grits are a Southern favorite made from ground hominy, which is corn with the hull and germ removed. Southerners traditionally serve grits with butter or chicken gravy, departing from the custom of eating cooked grains with sugar and milk or cream.

Quantities and Cooking Times

All cooked cereals and grains are prepared in a similar manner: they are stirred into boiling water, simmered for several minutes or more, then tightly covered and left over low heat to slowly absorb the cooking liquid. Cooking times

vary considerably depending on the degree of processing, the age, and the moisture content of the cereal. Some cereals, particularly whole cereals such as wheat berries, are soaked first, sometimes as long as overnight, to shorten the cooking time further.

The following shows the amount of water for cooking, the cooking time, and the yield for each cup of uncooked cereal.

Per Cup of Cereal	Water	Cooking Time	Yield
Brown rice	2 cups	45 to 60 minutes	3 cups
Buckwheat groats	2 to 2$^{1}/_{2}$ cups	10 to 12 minutes	2 to 2$^{1}/_{2}$ cups
Bulgur wheat	2 cups	15 minutes	2$^{1}/_{2}$ cups
Cracked wheat	2 cups	20 to 30 minutes	2 cups
Grits	5 cups	60 minutes	5 cups
Rolled oats	2 cups	5 to 10 minutes	2 cups
Steel-cut oats	2 cups	10 minutes	2 cups

Oatmeal

*This is the classic stick-to-your-ribs wintertime breakfast, a mother's
secret talisman for protecting children from draft, damp, and chill.
Was it really a surprise, then, to learn in recent years that oat bran has
unique properties that may help reduce the risk of heart disease? Mothers
know more than we think they do.*

SERVES 2 (MAKES 2 CUPS)

2 cups water, or 1 cup each water and milk
1/8 teaspoon salt
1 cup rolled or steel-cut oats

In a 2-quart saucepan, bring the water and salt to a boil (if
using milk, watch the pot closely to keep the milk from boiling
over). Stir in the oats, let the liquid return to a boil, and cook
for 3 minutes, stirring frequently. Cover the pan, reduce the
heat to very low, and cook for 5 more minutes, or until the
cooking liquid has been absorbed. Serve warm with cold milk,
sliced bananas, maple syrup, brown sugar, and/or butter.

   Two variations: Add one chopped, unpeeled apple or a
handful of raisins or quartered, pitted prunes with the dry
oatmeal. For a nuttier flavor, toast the uncooked oatmeal in
an oven at 400 degrees F. until it's light-brown, then cook
as usual.

After a night of festivity,
Germans long ago found
eating a bowl of oatmeal
topped with fried onions to
be an especially effective
hangover cure.

33

Toasted Three-Grain Cereal

Easy to cook on the spot, this cereal can also be cooked ahead of time, covered, and refrigerated for up to several days, then reheated by the bowlful for a last-minute hot breakfast. The toasty flavor goes especially well with real maple syrup.

SERVES 4 (MAKES 4 CUPS)

2/3 cups each steel-cut oats, bulgur wheat, and buckwheat
  groats
1/8 teaspoon salt

Preheat the oven to 400 degrees F. Spread the grains on a baking sheet and toast for about 10 minutes, stirring often, until golden brown. (You can double the quantity and make enough for later. Store tightly covered.)

In a 2-quart saucepan, bring 4 1/2 cups of water and the salt to a boil. Stir in the grains, let the water return to a boil, then cover the pan and simmer on low heat for 10 minutes, or until all the liquid is absorbed. Serve warm with a little cold milk or cream, sliced fruit, chopped nuts, brown sugar, or real maple syrup. Toasting enhances breakfast grains the way it enhances bread, producing a subtle crunchiness, a hint of smoky flavor, and a rich, golden color.

Southern Grits

Traditional Southern grits take a long time to cook, but they're worth the effort. Jim's grandmother, a native and resident of the Florida panhandle, remembers her mother starting the grits first thing in the morning, then pushing the pot to the back of the stove to cook slowly for up to several hours while she prepared the rest of the meal. Despite their rather unappetizing name, grits are wonderfully soft and creamy when prepared properly.

These days, Jim's grandma finds quick-cooking grits acceptable but avoids the instant variety. She serves grits alongside eggs and sausage or with fried chicken as part of a full Southern breakfast. She doesn't know what to think of Northerners who eat their grits with sugar and milk.

SERVES 4 TO 6

$^{1}/_{4}$ teaspoon salt
$^{3}/_{4}$ cup grits

Bring 4 cups of water and the salt to a boil in the top half of a double boiler. Stir in the grits. Place the pan over simmering water on medium-low heat in the bottom half of the double boiler. Cover and cook for 1 hour, stirring occasionally. When ready, the grits will be creamy and neither runny nor firm. Serve hot with plenty of butter or chicken gravy if you have it.

Leftover grits can be cut into half-inch slices, fried in butter until golden, and served with warm syrup, honey, or molasses.

Milk Toast

Enjoy this classic when no one is around. Not really a cereal in the technical sense of the word, this dish was originally conceived to baby the delicate constitution of the ill. It remains one of the ultimate breakfast comfort foods. Try it with cinnamon or raisin bread, brioche, or sweet French bread.

SERVES 1

2 slices of bread for toasting
2 tablespoons butter
1 tablespoon white sugar
3/4 cup cold milk

Toast and lightly butter the bread. While still warm, tear into bite-size pieces and place in a bowl. Sprinkle with sugar and pour on cold milk.

Cold Cereals for a Quick Start

Cold cereal helps us address one of the most pressing demands in the morning: limited time. Served with a minimum of preparation, it is among the most expeditious of breakfast foods. Of course, we pay a price for that convenience, both in dollars and cents and in terms of nutrition. Most of what's available is overpriced, overprocessed, and overly sweet.

Unlike hot cereals, for which the instant packaged versions are merely weak imitations, cold cereal is seldom made at home because so few home cooks can produce a satisfying facsimile of the commercially produced item. Yet homemade cold cereal is always cheaper and more nutritious, and with just a little advance planning, it's just as convenient. Below are recipes for two cold cereals to help meet the challenge of a fast, healthful breakfast.

Muesli

This is our version of an oat cereal created by Dr. Bircher-Benner, a nineteenth century Swiss nutritionist. Served chilled and moist, muesli prepared in the authentic manner offers an unusual and refreshing contrast to the warm softness and dry crunchiness we expect from breakfast grains. We chose apples and prunes for our version, but any combination of fresh and dried fruits will work.

SERVES 4 TO 6

1 1/2 cups old-fashioned rolled oats (not instant oats)
1 1/2 cups cold water, or 3/4 cup water and 3/4 cup
    unsweetened apple juice
2 apples (preferably Granny Smith), peeled and coarsely grated
1 1/2 cup pitted prunes, quartered or raisins or any dried fruit
3 tablespoons honey
juice of two lemons
1/2 teaspoon ground cinnamon
1/4 teaspoon ground nutmeg (preferably freshly ground)

In a large mixing bowl, combine all the ingredients thoroughly. The mixture will be fairly wet. Cover and refrigerate overnight. In the morning, serve a bowlful with sliced fruit, chopped nuts, yogurt, or milk. This cereal can be stored tightly covered in the refrigerator for a day or two.

Wheat has been cultivated as a cereal crop for at least 6,000 years.

37

Low-Fat Apple-and-Spice Granola

Just about the only cold cereal routinely made from scratch is granola, that culinary relic of the '60s. While a great source of fiber, traditional granola is also loaded with fat. Our version contains no added fat but every bit of the flavor.

SERVES 6 TO 8

2/3 cup frozen apple juice concentrate, thawed
2 tablespoons honey
1 tablespoon molasses
1 1/2 teaspoons vanilla extract
1/4 cup plus 2 tablespoons firmly packed brown sugar
1 tablespoon ground cinnamon
1/2 teaspoon ground ginger
4 cups old-fashioned rolled oats (not instant oats)
1/3 cup each coarsely chopped dried apples, dried currants, and
    dried cranberries
1/2 cup coarsely chopped toasted almonds

Preheat the oven to 400 degrees F. In a small saucepan, mix the juice concentrate, honey, molasses, vanilla, sugar, cinnamon, and ginger. Heat over medium heat, stirring with a wire whisk until the sugar melts and the ingredients are blended. Place the oats in a large mixing bowl and toss with the juice mixture to coat the grains completely.

Spread the oat mixture in a thin layer on one or more baking sheets with low sides, and place in the oven on the upper rack. Cook until golden brown, about 20 minutes, stirring every few minutes to prevent scorching. Remove from the oven and spread on another baking sheet to cool. When cooled, toss with the dried fruit and almonds. Serve with milk and fresh fruit or spooned over nonfat yogurt, or store tightly covered for up to several weeks.

"It takes some skill to spoil a breakfast—
even the English can't do it."

—John Kenneth Galbraith

"All happiness depends on a leisurely breakfast."

—John Gunther

3

PANCAKES, WAFFLES, AND MORE

Mastering the griddle may well be one of the most valuable of breakfast-time culinary skills. This single tool produces many wonderful foods, especially pancakes of all kinds, as well as waffles, French toast, crepes, and more.

Foods from the griddle comprise a large, diverse family, so that it almost seems easiest to define them by what they don't have in common. All rely on a pourable batter based on eggs and milk, but the similarities end there. Pancakes and waffles are a form of quick baking, with a batter that calls for chemical leavening agents, such as baking soda and baking powder, or natural leaveners like eggs and occasionally yeast. Crepes and oven pancakes are relatives of the popover, made from a thin batter that only relies on eggs for leavening. French toast is simply bread soaked in a mixture of eggs and milk; bread provides the structure, so flour, fat, and other ingredients aren't needed.

As for cooking methods, these dishes are all cooked directly against a hot surface, such as a traditional cast-iron frying pan or, nowadays, a nonstick skillet. This is the method of cooking originally described by the word "griddle," which is based on the word "grill." (To complicate matters, the British use the term "grill" to refer to a flat, hot cooking surface, whereas for Americans, a grill is for hamburgers.) In this sense, pancakes, French toast, waffles, and crepes are all *griddled*. Oven pancakes, which involve a batter almost identical to crepe batter,

also require a hot environment (the oven), producing results that are anything but flat.

What these treats do share in common is a tender texture, a beautiful golden color, and a pastry-like quality that makes an appealing, often dessert-like food. They are also enormously versatile. Savory versions of these dishes are found on lunch and dinner menus as well.

Pancakes and Waffles

Every culture produces its own version of flat bread: tortillas in Mexico, chapatis in India, pita throughout the Middle East, fry bread in the American Southwest. The pancakes most of us know arrived with Northern European immigrants, principally the Dutch, although the Germans, Scandinavians, and Finns brought similar versions, and the French introduced crepes. Even the ancient Romans made pancakes. Apicius, author of one of the earliest known books on cookery, includes a recipe for pancakes with the same ingredients we use today.

An indigenous American pancake, called the johnnycake, is a regular feature of breakfast in parts of New England. The Rhode Island Narragansett people shared this creation with European colonists in the early 1700s. Johnnycakes are traditionally made with cornmeal, salt, and either boiling water or

Every year since 1455, the residents of Olney, Buckinghamshire, England, have celebrated Shrove Tuesday as Pancake Day. The traditional festivities include a race in which women dressed as "housewives" flip a pancake, then run through town to the parish church carrying their skillets.

43

boiling milk, without fat, eggs, or other leavening agents commonly found in other pancakes; the result resembles cornbread in flavor and texture. The precise ingredients and methods of preparation remain a source of considerable debate and local pride.

The waffles we know arrived in America with the Dutch. This technique of cooking—baking a batter on or between irons inscribed with a design—was first use during the Middle Ages to make communion wafers. The French still produce something similar: the *gaufrette,* a thin, lightly sweetened, fan-shaped wafer served with ice cream or mousse.

Building a Better Batter

Both pancakes and waffles are made with essentially the same basic batter from ingredients commonly on hand in most kitchens. The technique is much easier than you might think. Food manufacturers have brainwashed many of us into believing that pancakes and waffles made from scratch are simply too much trouble. In fact, the basic technique is so simple that whipping up a batter from scratch takes no longer than preparing one from a mix—but what a difference in flavor and texture! After just a few tries, any pancake or waffle novice can be making them from scratch without even measuring. Here are some rules of thumb for successful pancakes and waffles:

- Use fresh ingredients, including fresh baking powder, which loses its punch with time. (You can make your own absolutely fresh baking powder by mixing 2 tablespoons of cream of tartar with 1 tablespoon of baking soda and 1 1/2 tablespoons of cornstarch.)

- Bring chilled ingredients, such as eggs and milk, to room temperature. Eggs whites are much easier to beat when they are warmer.

- If using melted butter, separate the eggs and mix the butter with the yolks. The emulsifying qualities of the yolk keep the melted butter from solidifying when it's added with the cooler liquid ingredients.

- Add wet ingredients to dry ingredients (not the other way around). A wire whisk works best for blending the ingredients. Only beat the batter long enough to blend the ingredients—lumps are OK. Too much stirring stimulates the formation of wheat gluten, the structures that give bread its chewiness. With pancakes and waffles, gluten just means toughness.

- Use the batter immediately unless otherwise directed (for example, crepe batter needs to rest). Pancakes and waffles are fluffy and light thanks to the carbon dioxide produced when acidic ingredients such as milk react with baking

soda or baking powder, but this reaction subsides quickly. Left to sit for very long, the bubbles dissipate, leaving the batter flat and lifeless.

✧ Pancakes and waffles are best eaten hot off the griddle or iron, but they can be kept warm for up to 15 minutes in an oven at 200 degrees F. Place one layer of pancakes or waffles on a baking pan or dish lined with a clean dish towel (preferably not one scented by a dryer sheet). Cover with another towel, then lay down another layer of cakes. The towels prevent drying while absorbing excess steam.

Perfect Pancakes

By using both milk and buttermilk, this recipe retains the tart richness of buttermilk but with the lightness that comes from milk. This batter could be used successfully for waffles, too.

MAKES 8 TO 10 PANCAKES, 3 INCHES EACH

1 cup all-purpose flour
1 tablespoon white sugar
$1/4$ teaspoon salt
$3/4$ teaspoon baking powder
$1/2$ teaspoon baking soda
1 egg

¹/₂ cup milk
³/₄ cup buttermilk
2 tablespoons unsalted butter

In a medium mixing bowl, stir together the flour, sugar, salt, baking powder, and baking soda (dry ingredients).

Separate the egg, placing the egg yolk in a small dish and the egg white in a medium bowl with the milk and buttermilk. Melt the butter in a 10- to 12-inch nonstick skillet over low heat, then add to the yolk and blend thoroughly. Stir the butter-yolk mixture into the milk mixture. Pour the wet ingredients all at once into the dry ingredients. Stir together briefly with a wire whisk (don't overmix— lumps are OK).

Increase the heat under the skillet to medium-high and, using a paper towel, brush the surface with a small bit of oil or melted butter. Pour in a scant ¹/₄ cup of batter for each pancake. As soon as large bubbles form and begin breaking on the facing surface (check the underside—it will be golden), flip the pancake and cook for another minute or two, or until you see little wisps of steam rise from the surface. Keep the skillet greased by adding small bits of butter and continue making pancakes.

Banana Pancakes

In a small mixing bowl, mash 1 ripe banana with a fork until smooth. Proceed with the pancake recipe above, adding $1/2$ teaspoon ground cloves to the dry ingredients. Blend the wet ingredients, then add the mashed banana, beating thoroughly until smooth. Complete the batter as directed.

Blueberry Pancakes

Follow the pancake recipe above, then gently fold $1/2$ cup fresh or frozen blueberries or sliced or mashed strawberries in the batter. Be careful not to stir any more than necessary. Add another spoonful of flour if the batter seems too thin.

Buttermilk Pancakes

Replace the milk with an equal amount of buttermilk, omit the baking powder, and increase the baking soda to a scant $2/3$ teaspoon. Complete the batter as directed in the pancake recipe above.

Oatmeal Pancakes

In medium bowl, stir 1 cup of old-fashioned rolled oats (not instant oats) into the milk and soak for 10 to 15 minutes. Meanwhile, prepare the remaining ingredients according to the pancake recipe above. Add the oatmeal-milk mixture to the other wet ingredients. Complete the batter as directed. Also try this variation with leftover cooked rice, granola, or lightly toasted, fresh breadcrumbs.

Cornmeal Pancakes

Substitute 1/2 cup yellow cornmeal for the flour in the pancake recipe above. Add 1 teaspoon of cinnamon to the dry ingredients, then complete the batter as directed.

German Oven Pancake

Few breakfast creations are quite as memorable as this one. This giant pancake emerges from the oven extravagantly puffed and golden. Show it to your guests immediately—like a soufflé, it begins to settle noticeably as it cools.

Sometimes called a Dutch baby pancake (actually a nickname for a smaller-sized version), this dish was introduced by a Seattle restaurant early in the century and later popularized by the West Coast's Sunset magazine in the late 1960s. Technically, this is not a pancake at all but a giant popover, a cousin of the crepe.

Use a low-sided baking dish no more than 3 inches deep. A large paella pan produces especially good results—the sloping sides cause the edges of the pancake to curl up and inward dramatically—but a large cast-iron skillet or a circular baking dish also works well. Our recipe calls for a 2- to 3-quart pan, but it can be adapted to larger pans, as described below.

SERVES 4

3 tablespoons unsalted butter
3 large eggs
³/₄ cup milk
³/₄ cup all-purpose flour
pinch salt
¹/₂ teaspoon vanilla extract
¹/₂ teaspoon finely grated lemon zest
1 tablespoon white sugar

Preheat the oven to 425 degrees F. Place the butter in a 2- to 3-quart cast-iron skillet or low-sided baking dish and place the dish in the oven. Working quickly as the butter melts, place the eggs in a blender jar and blend on high for 1 minute until frothy and light yellow. With the blender on, slowly add the milk, then the flour, and finally the remaining ingredients.

As soon as the butter melts (watch it so it doesn't burn), remove the pan from the oven, pour in the batter, and return pan to the oven for 20 to 25 minutes or until puffy and well browned (the exact time depends on the size of the pan). Cut into four wedges and serve as soon as possible. Top with a dusting of powdered sugar and a squeeze of lemon juice.

To make more than four servings, use a larger pan and adjust the recipe as follows: for each additional cup of capacity, add 1 egg, $1/4$ cup milk, $1/4$ cup flour, and 1 tablespoon butter.

Perfect Waffles

Any pancake batter can be successfully used to make waffles. However, waffle batter typically contains a little more oil and sugar to help the waffle brown and ensure a crispness that helps the waffle hold its shape. This additional structural integrity makes waffles easy to freeze and reheat in the toaster.

MAKES 8 TO 12 WAFFLES

1 cup all-purpose flour
2 tablespoons yellow cornmeal
1 tablespoon white sugar
$1/4$ teaspoon salt
$3/4$ teaspoon baking powder
$1/2$ teaspoon baking soda
1 egg
$1/2$ cup milk
$3/4$ cup buttermilk
4 tablespoons unsalted butter

Heat the waffle iron according to instructions. Meanwhile, in a medium mixing bowl, stir together the flour, cornmeal, sugar, salt, baking powder, and baking soda.

Separate the egg, placing the egg yolk in a small dish and the egg white in a second mixing bowl with the milk and buttermilk. Melt the butter in a 10- to 12-inch nonstick skillet over low heat, then add to the yolk and blend thoroughly. Stir the butter-yolk mixture into the milk mixture. Pour the wet ingredients all at once into the dry ingredients. With a wire whisk, stir together briefly (don't overmix—lumps are OK).

When the griddle is hot, pour in 1/2 to 3/4 cup of batter (the amount will vary with the size of the iron), and cook 7 to 8 minutes or until the waffle is golden brown. Serve warm with warm maple syrup, honey, fresh fruit, or other topping.

Wild Rice and Bacon Waffles

This rich waffle demands a tart, spicy topping, such as the Cranberry-Orange Sauce (page 60), although warm maple syrup (the real stuff) is also perfect. Serve these waffles for a cold-weather brunch. We can even envision serving them as a light supper, perhaps with sautéed mushrooms.

MAKES 8 TO 12 WAFFLES

4 slices bacon
1 1/4 cups all-purpose flour
1/4 cup cornmeal
1 1/2 teaspoons baking powder

¹/₂ teaspoon baking soda
¹/₂ teaspoon salt
1 tablespoon white sugar
8 tablespoons (1 stick) unsalted butter or vegetable oil
3 eggs, separated
1 cup buttermilk
³/₄ cup whole or low-fat milk
¹/₄ cup cooked wild rice

In an 8- to 10-inch nonstick skillet, fry the bacon over low heat until crisp. Drain and cool on paper towels, then crumble into small pieces. Stir the flour, cornmeal, baking powder, baking soda, salt, and sugar together in a medium bowl.

Melt the butter in a small skillet or saucepan over low heat, then blend thoroughly with the egg yolks. Stir the butter-yolk mixture into the buttermilk and milk. Add the wet ingredients to the dry ingredients and briefly mix with a whisk (lumps are OK). Stir in the wild rice and bacon. Whip the egg whites with a wire whisk or handheld electric mixer until stiff but not dry. Fold into the batter.

Heat the waffle iron according to instructions. Pour in ¹/₂ to ³/₄ cup of batter (the amount will vary with the size of the iron), and cook 7 to 8 minutes or until golden brown.

Blueberry Waffles

To the basic waffle batter (page 49), fold in $1/2$ cup of fresh or frozen blueberries. Prepare as directed.

Crepes

Crepes are French pancakes made with a thin batter that contains no leavening agents such as yeast, baking soda, or baking powder. Actually, the French produce several kinds of crepes. The Parisian variety, the one familiar to most of us, is thin, delicate, and pale and is usually served with a filling as a brunch dish, light supper, or even dessert. The residents of Brittany, on the northern Atlantic coast, prepare more robust crepes the size of large platters using a heavier batter made with whole wheat or buckwheat flour. Either type is spread with jam or sprinkled with sugar and folded in quarters to be eaten by hand, often as a take-out treat.

Producing the thin, almost papery texture for the crepes described below requires just a bit of practice. Use less batter than you think you need, and keep a supple wrist when spreading the batter in the pan.

MAKES 16 TO 20 (6-INCH) CREPES

1 cup all-purpose flour
$2/3$ cup whole or low-fat milk
3 eggs
2 tablespoons vegetable oil
$1/4$ teaspoon salt

In a blender, place flour, $3/4$ cup water, milk, eggs, oil, and salt, and blend on high until smooth. Cover and refrigerate for at

To season a cast-iron skillet, coat it with unseasoned shortening and place it in an oven at 350 degrees F. for two hours. Cool and wipe thoroughly with a paper towel before using.

least one hour. Remove from the refrigerator and blend for one more minute.

Heat over medium-high heat a 6-inch crepe pan or large nonstick skillet with a flat bottom 6 inches across. Brush the pan lightly with some vegetable oil. Add approximately 1/4 cup of batter and quickly turn and tilt the pan to make the batter completely cover the bottom surface. Cook until the top loses its shininess and looks somewhat dry. Carefully turn with a small nonstick or wooden spatula. Cook the other side briefly, just until lightly golden. Stack the crepes on a warm plate and cover them with a clean dish towel until ready to serve.

Serve with the filling of your choice or roll loosely and sprinkle with a little powdered sugar and a squeeze of fresh lemon juice. When cooled, unfilled crepes can be stacked, wrapped tightly in plastic, and frozen. Allow frozen crepes to defrost completely before filling.

Crepes with Apple or Pear Filling

Though designed for breakfast, this filling could just as easily be served as dessert. For example, dress up these crepes with a dusting of powdered sugar or a dollop of whipped cream. (We might even try spooning the filling itself over a slice of pound cake.)

SERVES 4

Never wash a seasoned skillet. Instead, scour it with a pot scrubber or with a dampened sponge sprinkled liberally with coarse salt. Rinse with hot water and dry immediately.

8 tablespoons (1 stick) unsalted butter
6 apples or pears, peeled, cored, and
    sliced 1/4-inch thick
3/4 cup brown sugar
1 teaspoon salt
1/4 teaspoon ground cinnamon
1/4 teaspoon ground nutmeg
1 cup raisins
1/2 cup apple juice
6 crepes (page 54)

In a 10- to 12-inch nonstick skillet, melt the butter over
medium-high heat. Add the fruit, sugar, salt, cinnamon,
nutmeg, and raisins and cook until the fruit is golden. Add
the juice and continue to cook until heated through.

To assemble, place 1 crepe in a 9 × 13-inch baking pan.
Place 3/4 cup of the filling and about 1/4 cup of the sauce
across the middle section of the crepe, then gently roll it up
so the ends are tucked underneath. Repeat with the remaining
crepes, placing each one next to the others. Once all the
crepes are filled, place in the oven to heat through, about
5 minutes. Remove from the oven, place two crepes on each
serving place and pour the remaining sauce over the top.
Serve immediately.

Chicken Crepes with Madeira Sauce

This filling is lovely and fragrant. These crepes are extra special served with a fruit salad and champagne.

SERVES 4

6 tablespoons unsalted butter
1 tablespoon minced yellow onion
1/2 cup pecans, chopped
3 1/2 cups heavy cream
3 1/2 cups chicken stock, preferably homemade or low-salt
1 cup Madeira
2 pounds poached chicken, skinned and torn into
    bite-size pieces
1 teaspoon each salt and freshly ground black pepper
8 crepes (page 54)

Preheat the oven to 325 degrees F. In a 10- to 12-inch non-stick skillet, melt the butter over medium-high heat. Add the onion and pecans and cook until golden. Set aside.

    In a separate 10- to 12-inch nonstick skillet, heat the cream, stock, and Madeira over medium-high heat and cook until reduced by one-third. Reduce the heat to low, and add the chicken and onion-pecan mixture. Add salt and pepper and heat through.

    Assemble the crepes as described on the opposite page.

French Toast

The French call this breakfast favorite pain perdu *or "lost bread," because it's ideal for using up day-old bread (in fact, fresh bread works rather poorly when used in this recipe). Different types of bread produce different textures and flavors. Our favorites include sourdough bread and any chewy, crusty peasant-style loaf. If you can find it, try challah or brioche, which produce an especially rich French toast.*

SERVES 4 TO 6

2 eggs plus 1 egg white
1 1/2 cups whole or low-fat milk
1/2 teaspoon cinnamon
1 teaspoon vanilla extract (or the seeds scraped from a 4-inch
    section of vanilla bean)
8 to 12 slices of any day-old bread, preferably sliced thickly
3 to 4 tablespoons unsalted butter

In a mixing bowl large enough to hold 2 to 3 slices of bread, vigorously beat the eggs, egg white, milk, cinnamon, and vanilla until frothy. Place 2 or 3 slices of bread in the bowl and turn to coat with the mixture. Leave to soak for several minutes or until the bread is thoroughly soaked but not mushy.

Meanwhile, melt 1 tablespoon of the butter in a 10-inch nonstick skillet over medium-high heat. Add the soaked bread slices. Cook each side for 3 to 4 minutes or until golden, adding more butter as you go in case the pan seems dry. Repeat with the remaining bread. Serve warm with warm syrup or dusted with powdered sugar and fresh fruit.

For extra-custardy French toast: the night before, cut the bread into thick slices, lay them in a single layer in a baking dish, and pour the milk-egg mixture over them. Cover and refrigerate overnight. The next morning, proceed as directed above.

Orange French Toast

In the basic recipe above, substitute 1 cup freshly squeezed orange juice (or 1/2 cup each orange juice and Grand Marnier) for 1 cup of the milk. Add the finely grated zest of one orange. Proceed with the recipe as directed.

Syrups, Sauces, and Toppings

Maple syrup may well be the only food truly native to North America. Though the sugar maple (*Acer saccharum*) will grow elsewhere, only in the climate of New England and neighboring areas of Canada does the tree produce the sap that becomes maple syrup and maple sugar.

Until European colonists introduced the Italian honeybee in 1625, maple syrup and maple sugar were the only concentrated sweeteners available in North America. They remained the

On average, it takes 35 gallons of sugar maple sap to produce one gallon of maple syrup. The average tree produces 12 gallons of sap per season.

59

Northeast's major sweetener until the late nineteenth century, when cane and beet sugar became much cheaper to produce.

We firmly believe that just about any food tastes better with maple syrup—the real stuff. If you're only accustomed to store-bought pancake syrup (which is basically caramel-flavored corn syrup, with little if any real maple flavor), you'll be delighted with the delicate sweetness and light texture of the real item. Don't balk at the rather steep price—this is definitely a luxury. If you can't afford much, buy the largest amount of the best quality you can afford and save it for special occasions (check with local health food stores, which often sell maple syrup in bulk).

Cranberry-Orange Sauce

The tartness of cranberries and orange and the subtle heat of fresh ginger are nice foils for the richness of most pancakes, waffles, and French toast.

MAKES 2 CUPS

12 ounces fresh or frozen cranberries
2 teaspoons fresh orange zest
2 tablespoons finely chopped fresh ginger
1 cup frozen cranberry juice concentrate, thawed
1/2 cup white sugar
juice of four medium oranges (about 1 1/2 cups)

Combine all the ingredients in a heavy, nonreactive 1 1/2-quart saucepan. Cover and heat over medium-high, stirring occasionally and mashing the cranberries against the side of the pan. Continue stirring until thick and fairly smooth. Thin with a little water if the mixture becomes too thick. Serve warm or let cool completely, then refrigerate tightly covered for up to two weeks.

Honeyed Apricot Sauce

Mild honey cuts the tartness of this puree of stewed dried apricots. A spoonful is great stirred into nonfat plain yogurt.

MAKES ABOUT 1 1/2 CUPS

1/2 cup dried apricots
1/2 cup mild honey

Place the apricots and 1 1/2 cups water in a medium saucepan. Bring to a boil, then reduce the heat to low and cover the pan. Simmer for 7 to 10 minutes or until the fruit is very soft and water is partly absorbed. Remove from the heat and let cool for 5 minutes.

Pour into a food processor work bowl fitted with a steel blade and add the honey. Pulse briefly and repeatedly until the mixture is a partly smooth puree. Return to the saucepan and simmer for 3 to 4 minutes, stirring often. Serve warm or refrigerate tightly covered for up to a week.

Americans today annually consume just one-fourth the amount of maple syrup they consumed a hundred years ago.

Spiced Apple Syrup

This spicy dark syrup is the essence of mulled cider.

MAKES 1 CUP

2 cups unsweetened apple juice, preferably unfiltered
4 tablespoons brown sugar
1 piece (2 inches) whole cinnamon
3 whole cloves
1 allspice berry (optional)

Bring all the ingredients to a boil in a medium nonreactive saucepan. Reduce the heat to medium-low and simmer for 30 to 40 minutes, or until reduced to 1 cup. Serve warm or refrigerate tightly covered for up to a week.

Fresh Strawberry-Banana Sauce

Banana puree sweetens this sauce of mashed strawberries. This recipe contains no added sugar or fat.

MAKES 2 CUPS

2 baskets strawberries, washed, hulled, and sliced
1 ripe banana, sliced

Place the sliced strawberries in a medium nonreactive mixing bowl. Using a wire whisk, gently mash the berries to a coarse puree (chunks are OK). In a separate small bowl, mash the banana completely and stir into the berries. Serve immediately.

4

BREAKFAST BAKING

When a recipe calls for buttermilk, soured milk makes a fine emergency substitute. Measure an equal amount of sweet milk, then for each cup, add 1 tablespoon of cider vinegar. Set it aside for several minutes before using. No other adjustments to your recipe are needed.

Compared to other forms of breakfast cookery, baking calls for some advanced planning and a modicum of skill and confidence. Food manufacturers have exploited this fact to sell the convenience of mixes and packaged products. The truth is, anyone who can measure and mix can bake from scratch for breakfast.

The Chemistry of Breakfast Baking

Fully appreciating the simplicity of baking in the morning requires the briefest introduction to culinary chemistry. Consider a basic loaf of sandwich bread. The dough gets its lift from the carbon dioxide bubbles naturally produced by yeasts as they metabolize sugars. The process cannot be rushed—bread dough requires anywhere from several hours to several days to rise.

By contrast, most breakfast-time baking relies on the chemical reaction between the acidic components of milk or buttermilk and the alkaline components of baking soda or baking powder, which produces carbon dioxide bubbles almost immediately. We already observe this reaction when making pancakes (really just another form of simple baking)— you see the batter begin to bubble right before your eyes.

This quick rise is what makes breakfast baking so simple and therefore so practical.

But don't overlook the fact that baking is also pleasant and peaceful. Done in the evening after dinner is finished and the house is growing quiet, breakfast baking affords the opportunity for thoughtful, calm concentration—really almost a form of meditation.

Bran Muffins

The ultimate do-ahead recipe: this batter will last in the refrigerator, tightly covered, for up to six weeks. Try sprinkling the top of each muffin with a tablespoon of chopped walnuts before baking.

MAKES 24 MUFFINS

6 1/2 cups 40% bran flakes cereal
1 1/2 cups white sugar
2 1/2 cups all-purpose flour
2 1/2 teaspoons baking soda
1 teaspoon salt
1 cup raisins
1/2 cup vegetable oil
2 eggs
2 cups buttermilk

In a large mixing bowl, stir together the cereal, sugar, flour, baking soda, salt, and raisins. In a separate bowl, mix together the oil, eggs, and buttermilk. Stir the wet ingredients into the dry ingredients and blend thoroughly. Cover and refrigerate overnight.

Preheat the oven to 375 degrees F. Lightly grease muffin tins with vegetable shortening and fill halfway with the batter. Bake 20 to 25 minutes or until the muffin springs back when lightly pressed.

Molly's Gingerbread Muffins

If you can resist eating them when they're fresh from the oven, keep these muffins hidden away in the freezer for unexpected guests or an irresistible craving. Since the aroma of gingerbread conjures up images of Christmas trees and snow, we take special pleasure in making these muffins during the sweltering summer months to serve with fresh strawberries and a glass of freshly squeezed orange juice.

MAKES 12 MUFFINS

2 cups all-purpose bleached flour
1 teaspoon baking soda
1 teaspoon baking powder
1 teaspoon ground ginger
1/4 teaspoon ground cinnamon

$^1/_8$ teaspoon ground allspice
$^1/_2$ cup white sugar
8 tablespoons (1 stick) unsalted butter, at room temperature
2 eggs, at room temperature
$^1/_2$ cup dark molasses
$^1/_2$ cup whole or low-fat milk, at room temperature
$^1/_4$ cup dried currants, soaked for 5 minutes in hot water,
     then drained well
$^1/_2$ cup chopped walnuts

Preheat the oven to 425 degrees F. Lightly grease a standard muffin tin with vegetable shortening. In a medium bowl, sift together the flour, baking soda, baking powder, ginger, cinnamon, and allspice. Set aside.

With an electric beater, cream together the sugar and butter until light and fluffy. Add the eggs one at a time. Add the molasses and milk. Beat well. Add the flour mixture and mix until just blended. Fold in the currants and walnuts. Fill muffin tins $^3/_4$ full. Bake for 18 minutes or until a toothpick inserted in the center of a muffin comes out clean.

Tip: An ice cream scoop is a great tool for spooning equal portions of batter into each muffin tin.

Make your own baking powder by mixing 1 tablespoon of baking soda with 2 tablespoons of cream of tartar and 1$^1/_2$ tablespoons of cornstarch (for larger quantities, these amounts can be increased proportionately). Use your baking powder as you would the commercial variety. Store for up to a month in a tightly sealed jar.

Biscuit Basics

Biscuits are one of the quickest baked goods to prepare for breakfast. The basic ingredients couldn't be simpler and neither is the technique. Achieving a properly tender biscuit requires the lightest possible touch. Too much handling encourages the formation of wheat gluten, which gives baked goods their chewiness—not a desirable trait in biscuits.

Biscuits come in two basic forms: rolled and drop. They use almost identical batter (dropped biscuit batter is slightly more moist). To make rolled biscuits, the batter is rolled flat and cut like pie or cookie dough. As the name indicates, drop biscuits are formed by dropping the batter in spoonfuls onto the baking sheet.

When cutting dough for biscuits, be sure the cutter has a sharp edge. A dull edge will seal the edge of the dough and inhibit rising.

Rolled Biscuits

Nothing is lighter than a perfectly made rolled biscuit. The delicate layers are just right for a little butter, jam, or honey.

MAKES 10 TO 12 BISCUITS

2 cups all-purpose flour
1/2 teaspoon salt
4 teaspoons baking powder
6 tablespoons solid shortening
2/3 cup milk

Preheat the oven to 450 degrees F. In a medium mixing bowl, sift together the flour, salt, and baking powder. Using a pastry cutter or your fingers, lightly blend in the shortening until the mixture resembles coarse cornmeal (but not any finer—the moisture in the tiny chunks of butter helps the biscuits rise). Make a well in the center of the mixture. Pour in the milk all at once and with a mixing spoon stir firmly and quickly (no more than 30 seconds) to blend. The batter will come together in the bowl.

Turn the batter out onto a lightly floured surface, briefly knead for just one or two turns, and pat into a circle 1/2-inch thick. Prick the surface with a fork. Using a sharp floured biscuit cutter, cut out 10 to 12 biscuits. Place on an ungreased baking sheet and bake for 10 to 12 minutes until lightly browned. Serve hot.

69

Have you ever struggled to accurately measure solid shortening? Next time, try the displacement method. To measure $1/3$ cup shortening, for example, fill a 1-cup measuring cup with $2/3$ cup water, then spoon in shortening until the water rises to 1 cup. This method works for any quantity of shortening. Pour off the water (it won't affect the shortening), then proceed with your recipe.

Drop Biscuits

Made even more quickly than rolled biscuits, these biscuits have an especially rustic, homey feel to them.

MAKES 10 TO 12 BISCUITS

2 cups all-purpose flour
$1/2$ teaspoon salt
4 teaspoons baking powder
6 tablespoons solid shortening
1 cup milk

Preheat the oven to 450 degrees F. In a medium mixing bowl, sift together the flour, salt, and baking powder. Using a pastry cutter or your fingers, lightly blend in the shortening until the mixture resembles coarse cornmeal (but not any finer—the moisture in the tiny chunks of butter helps the biscuits rise). Make a well in the center of the mixture. Pour in the milk all at once and with a mixing spoon stir firmly and quickly (no more than 30 seconds) to blend.

The batter will be soft and quite moist. Drop in large spoonfuls onto an ungreased baking sheet. Bake for 10 to 12 minutes or until lightly browned. Serve hot.

Note: Either biscuit recipe can be made using buttermilk, which can replace the milk cup for cup. However, buttermilk in the recipe requires baking soda in place of baking powder. When using buttermilk in the recipes above, use 1 teaspoon of baking soda in place of the baking powder.

Cream and Cranberry Scones

*Scones are biscuits enriched with eggs and cream. Karletta first made
these particular scones with her childhood friend, Elizabeth, years
before scones became a sensation. You might try using dried cherries
or currants instead of dried cranberries.*

MAKES 8 SCONES

2 cups all-purpose flour
1 tablespoon baking powder
2 tablespoons plus 2 teaspoons white sugar
$^1/_2$ teaspoon salt
4 tablespoons chilled unsalted butter, cut into several pieces
$^1/_2$ cup dried cranberries
2 eggs, beaten slightly
$^1/_2$ teaspoon vanilla or almond extract
$^1/_3$ cup heavy cream
1 egg white, beaten

Scones are supposedly
named for the Stone of
Destiny (the Scone), at
which Scottish kings were
crowned.

Preheat the oven to 400 degrees F. Place the flour, baking
powder, 2 tablespoons of the sugar, salt, and butter in a food
processor work bowl fitted with a steel blade. Pulse repeatedly
until the mixture resembles small peas. (If you do not have a
food processor, simply place these ingredients into a bowl and
cut the butter into the flour using two dinner knives.) Pour the
mixture into a medium mixing bowl with the cranberries. Stir
the two eggs, vanilla, and cream into the mixture.

Turn the dough out onto a floured board and knead until it
sticks together. Roll into a ball and pat it out into a circle about

71

1-inch thick. Cut into 8 equal wedges. Place each wedge on a baking sheet lined with baker's parchment. Brush each wedge with the beaten egg white, then sprinkle with the remaining 2 teaspoons sugar. Bake for approximately 15 minutes or until lightly browned. Serve warm.

Raspberry Coffee Cake

The tartness of the raspberries contrast nicely with the sweetness of the topping and glaze. This coffee cake is best served the same morning it is prepared, as the berries can turn soggy overnight.

SERVES 6 TO 8

The topping:

1/3 cup white sugar
1 cup all-purpose flour
8 tablespoons (1 stick) chilled unsalted butter, cut into
    1/2-inch pieces

The cake:

8 tablespoons (1 stick) unsalted butter, cut into
    6 to 8 pieces
1 cup white sugar
2 eggs
1 teaspoon vanilla extract
1/4 teaspoon nutmeg
1 tablespoon baking powder
2 1/3 cups all-purpose flour

Not sure whether your baking powder is still fresh? Stir 1 teaspoon into 1/3 cup hot water. If it bubbles vigorously, it's still fresh.

1 cup milk
2 cups fresh raspberries

The glaze:
1/4 cup powdered sugar
2 tablespoons cold water

Preheat the oven to 350 degrees F.

Prepare the topping: Combine the sugar, flour, and butter in a food processor work bowl fitted with a steel blade. Pulse repeatedly until the mixture resembles small peas. Set aside. (If you do not have a food processor, simply place the topping ingredients into a bowl and cut the butter into the flour using two dinner knives.)

Prepare the cake: In the bowl of an electric mixer, cream the butter and sugar. Add the eggs, vanilla, nutmeg, and baking powder and continue to beat for 4 minutes. Meanwhile, in a small saucepan, warm the milk over very low heat. Add 1 cup of the flour and 1/3 cup of the milk to the bowl and beat until smooth. Add the rest of the flour and milk and beat for 1 more minute. Pour the batter into a buttered and floured 10-inch springform pan. Sprinkle the berries and the topping mixture on top of the batter. Bake for 1 1/4 hours or until the top is lightly browned.

Meanwhile, prepare the glaze: In a small mixing bowl, stir together the sugar and water until smooth. When the cake is done and still warm, drizzle it with the glaze. Serve warm.

Sour Cream Coffee Cake

There is nothing as welcoming to friends as a freshly baked coffee cake. This recipe has been in Karletta's family for years. It's a wonderful cake to just have around the house, waiting for unexpected company—if it lasts that long!

SERVES 8 TO 10

8 tablespoons (1 stick) unsalted butter, at room temperature
1 cup plus 1 1/2 tablespoons white sugar
2 eggs
1 cup sour cream
1 teaspoon vanilla extract
1 1/2 cups all-purpose flour
1 teaspoon baking powder
1 teaspoon baking soda
1/2 teaspoon salt
1 cup walnuts, chopped
1 teaspoon cinnamon

Preheat the oven to 350 degrees F. In a medium bowl, cream the butter, 1 cup of the sugar, and eggs with an electric mixer. Add the sour cream and vanilla and beat until fully incorporated. In a separate bowl, sift together the flour, baking powder, baking soda, and salt. Add to the butter-sugar mixture and beat until well blended. Stir in the walnuts, cinnamon, and the remaining 1 1/2 tablespoons sugar. Pour into a greased angel food cake pan. Bake for 45 minutes or until a toothpick inserted into the cake comes out clean. Cool slightly, about 10 minutes. Run a short, sharp knife between the cake and pan to loosen, then invert onto a wire baking rack.

Recipes for muffins, biscuits, and other quick breads usually call for either milk and baking powder or buttermilk and baking soda. You can substitute buttermilk for milk cup for cup, but replace the baking powder with one-fourth the amount of baking soda. This formula also applies in reverse when substituting milk for buttermilk: replace the baking soda with four times as much baking powder.

5

MEAT AND POTATOES

Mainstays at the American dinner table, meat and potatoes serve somewhat different roles at breakfast. Bacon, sausage, or ham, the most common breakfast meats, generally accompany other dishes such as eggs or pancakes and offer a salty, sizzling, toothsome contrast to the creaminess and sweetness of these foods. The potato is also an accompaniment at breakfast, where its warm, filling, comforting qualities are particularly favored.

Serving Meat for Breakfast

The conventions governing breakfast are rather specific when it comes to meat. Beef and fish seldom appear on the traditional breakfast menu, although in the form of steak and eggs, lox and bagels, or pan-fried trout (ideally caught at sunrise and cooked over a campfire) they are among the most memorable of breakfast meats. If poultry appears at all, it's typically featured as chicken hash, although increasingly as sausage, too.

Pork—or more precisely, salt- or smoke-cured pork—rules the breakfast table. Indeed, with the power to penetrate closed bedroom doors and the snuggest cocoon of bedding, the aroma and sizzle of frying bacon signal breakfast-time at any hour of the day.

That pork is a traditional part of the American breakfast is a historical remnant. Until this century, in a time when a sub-

stantial breakfast was necessary for facing a long day in the field, forest, or foundry, pork was the most widely consumed meat in America. Before the advent of refrigeration, of course, any fresh meat that was not consumed immediately had to be cured for later use. As a breakfast food, cured meat offers the advantage of being easily cooked with little additional preparation (suggesting that time constraints at breakfast are nothing new). These days, bacon is universally associated with breakfast. Ham, usually fried, is a country favorite still common at Southern tables. Many kinds of sausage appear at breakfast-time, from the familiar German, Polish, and Italian varieties to chorizo, the spicy Mexican pork sausage that goes so well with eggs.

Tips for Cooking Bacon

- ❖ Whether frying or broiling, always start with a cold pan. This keeps the bacon from curling.

- ❖ Cook slowly over medium heat and watch the pan closely, as bacon burns very quickly.

- ❖ Don't crowd the pan. Otherwise, the bacon will steam, not fry. Cook in batches if necessary.

- ❖ Prepare and serve Canadian bacon, which is the eye of loin, as you would ham.

"Elizabeth Tudor her breakfast would make, On a pot of strong beef and a pound of beefsteak, Ere six in the morning was tolled by the chimes— Oh, the days of Queen Bess, they were doughty old times!"

—Anonymous (1900)

Chicken: The Other Sausage Meat

Chicken seems to appear at every meal these days, in the morning most notably as sausage. This is good news for the health conscious: chicken sausage has only about half the fat of sausage made from pork.

Sausage is one of those foods very few people make at home, which is unfortunate. Dispense with the sausage casings, and it's really no more difficult to make than meat loaf.

One excellent technique for homemade chicken sausage comes from Bruce Aidells, a San Francisco-based sausage maker who led a modern resurgence in this traditional culinary art and pioneered the production of poultry sausage. His method calls for using a food processor in place of the butcher's meat grinder.

The key is to freeze the meat before grinding it. This gives the sausage a pleasingly coarse texture and ensures an even blend of meat and fat (juiciness depends on at least some fat). From there, the preparations involve just a little measuring and mixing.

The two recipes below call for chicken thighs, which have enough fat to afford the right degree of juiciness (breast meat is too lean). Turkey can be substituted as well.

Sweet Italian Chicken Sausage

This sausage has a delicate, herbaceous flavor. White wine keeps it moist.

MAKES ABOUT 2 POUNDS

2 pounds boneless chicken thighs, including skin (about
    4 pounds with bones)
1 1/2 teaspoons minced garlic
2 tablespoons chopped fresh Italian parsley
1/2 teaspoon each dried oregano and thyme leaves
1 1/2 teaspoons fennel seed
3/4 teaspoon black pepper
1/4 teaspoon cayenne
1 1/2 teaspoons salt
1/2 cup white wine

If it isn't boneless, bone the chicken thighs (or have the butcher do it), reserving the skin. Cut the meat and skin into 1-inch pieces. Spread them in one layer on a baking sheet lined with wax paper or foil and place in the freezer for about 30 minutes or until the meat is quite firm. Alternatively, freeze the thighs whole and cut them into 1-inch pieces while still frozen.

    Place the remaining ingredients in a large mixing bowl. Place the chicken in a food processor work bowl fitted with a steel blade. Working in several batches, pulse the meat and skin

Abraham Lincoln's two favorite breakfasts consisted of ham, cream gravy, and biscuits and fried apples with salt pork.

repeatedly until the pieces are roughly 3/8 inch in size (avoid overprocessing). Place each batch in the mixing bowl. Using your hands, blend the ingredients thoroughly. The wine will make the sausage mixture feel fairly wet. (For sanitary reasons, work quickly to prevent the chicken from warming up.)

Heat a small skillet over medium-high heat and cook a small amount of sausage to test the seasonings. Adjust them accordingly. Serve as you would traditional pork sausage. Keep the sausage wrapped tightly in the refrigerator for two days or freeze for up to two months.

Creole Chicken Sausage

Chilies, garlic, and herbs give this spicy sausage an authentic New Orleans bite.

MAKES ABOUT 2 POUNDS

2 pounds boneless chicken thighs, including skin
    (about 4 pounds with bone)
1/2 medium yellow onion (about 1/4 pound), chopped
1 1/2 teaspoons minced fresh jalapeño pepper
1/4 teaspoon minced garlic
1/4 teaspoon (scant) dried thyme leaves
1 teaspoon finely chopped fresh Italian parsley
1 bay leaf (dried), center vein removed and crushed finely
1/4 teaspoon chili powder

$^1/_2$ teaspoon paprika
$^1/_4$ teaspoon cayenne
1 teaspoon ground black pepper
1 teaspoon salt
$1^1/_2$ teaspoons red wine vinegar

Prepare the chicken for grinding according to the recipe for Sweet Italian Chicken Sausage. Grind the chicken and skin along with the chopped onion, as described in the previous recipe. Place the remaining ingredients in a large mixing bowl, then add the chicken.

Using your hands, blend the ingredients thoroughly. Heat a small skillet over medium-high heat and cook a small amount of sausage to test the seasonings. Adjust them accordingly. Serve as you would traditional pork sausage. Keep the sausage wrapped tightly in the refrigerator for two days or freeze for up to two months.

Potatoes for Breakfast

The potato is the inevitable accompaniment to meat at the dinner table, but it takes on a life of its own at breakfast. With only a little trouble, last night's uneaten baked or boiled potatoes become this morning's home fries or hash browns.

Hash Browns

You'll never lack for a comforting meal with potatoes in the house. We can make a meal anytime out of hash browns and a green salad.

SERVES 6

4 large russet potatoes (about 2 1/2 pounds)
1/2 teaspoon white vinegar
1/2 teaspoon each salt and freshly ground black pepper
2 tablespoons unsalted butter
3 tablespoons vegetable oil
1 teaspoon chopped fresh Italian parsley

In a large nonreactive pot, cook the potatoes in boiling salted water with the vinegar for about 20 minutes—the potatoes will still be firm. Drain and refrigerate overnight (this ensures a golden crust). The next morning, peel the potatoes and grate them into a large mixing bowl. Toss them with the salt and pepper.

Heat a 10- to 12-inch nonstick skillet over medium-high heat and melt the butter along with the oil. Add the potatoes and pat into a single large, flat cake using a spatula. Reduce the heat to medium-low and cook until a golden brown crust forms on the bottom. Turn over and brown the other side.

Divide into four wedges, top with the parsley, and serve warm from the pan.

The potato was imported from Peru to Spain in the 1530's, reached Ireland via the first Virginia colony in the 1580's, and finally arrived in America in 1719 with Irish immigrants.

Home Fries

These potatoes are very good served alongside all egg dishes. Make them even more special by topping them with a dollop of sour cream and chopped green onion. Refrigerating the potatoes overnight helps them to cook more crisply.

SERVES 4

4 large russet potatoes (about 2 1/2 pounds)
3 tablespoons unsalted butter
3 tablespoons vegetable oil
1/4 cup each chopped green pepper, red pepper, and
    yellow onion
Salt, pepper, and paprika to taste

Clean the potatoes well by scrubbing their skins with a vegetable brush. Cook in boiling salted water for about 20 minutes—they will still be firm. Drain and refrigerate overnight. The next day, cut the potatoes into 1 1/2-inch cubes, leaving their skins on.

Heat a 10- to 12-inch nonstick skillet over medium-high heat and melt the butter along with the oil. Add the green pepper, red pepper, and onion and cook for 5 minutes. Add the potatoes and season to taste with the salt, pepper, and paprika. Continue cooking, turning frequently to brown the potatoes on all sides. Adjust the seasonings, if necessary, and serve warm.

Brunch Potatoes

These French-inspired potatoes work well accompanied by (or even topped with) a couple of poached eggs.

SERVES 4 TO 6

2 teaspoons minced shallots
3 tablespoons red wine vinegar
2 teaspoons minced garlic
2 teaspoons grated lemon zest
1/2 cup olive oil
salt and black pepper to taste
3 pounds red or white boiling potatoes, peeled, cut into
     1/4-inch slices, and patted dry
1/2 cup fresh Italian parsley, chopped

Preheat the oven to 200 degrees F. In a small nonreactive saucepan, bring the shallots, vinegar, garlic, and lemon zest to a boil. Reduce the heat to medium and simmer for 3 minutes. Remove from the heat and whisk in 1/4 cup of the olive oil. Season to taste with the salt and pepper and set aside.

In a 10-inch to 12-inch nonstick skillet, heat 2 table-spoons of the remaining olive oil over medium heat. Add enough of the potato slices to make a single layer across the bottom of the pan—do not crowd the slices, or they won't brown. Turning them occasionally, cook until golden brown on both sides. Remove from the pan to a large heat-proof bowl and keep warm, covered, in the oven. Repeat with the remaining oil and potato slices until all the potatoes have been cooked.

Place the remaining potatoes in the bowl. Pour the warm vinegar mixture over them and toss gently. Add the parsley, toss again, and serve immediately.

Chicken Hash

When we enjoy a roasted chicken for dinner on Saturday nights, we know that come Sunday morning the leftovers will become this very easy hash. Boiling the potatoes the night before (for example, while the chicken roasts) shortens the assembly time the next morning.

SERVES 4

1 cup russet potatoes, peeled, cubed, boiled, and drained completely
1 1/2 cups cooked chicken, torn into bite-size pieces
1/2 teaspoon poultry seasoning
1 teaspoon fresh thyme leaves, chopped
1/2 teaspoon each salt and freshly ground black pepper
3 tablespoons vegetable oil
2 tablespoons thinly sliced green onions

Because it is a member of the nightshade family, the potato was originally suspect to Europeans, who mistakenly considered it to be poisonous. Sir Walter Raleigh helped to dispel this notion by planting potatoes on his farm in Ireland in the 1580's.

87

In a medium bowl, lightly mash the potatoes with a fork, leaving large lumps. Add the chicken, seasoning, thyme, salt, and pepper and mix thoroughly. The mixture will be loose.

Heat the oil in a 10- to 12-inch nonstick skillet over medium-high heat. Add the hash mixture and pat into a single large, flat cake using a spatula. Cook until a golden brown crust forms on the bottom. Turn over and brown the other side.

Divide into four wedges and place on four warm plates. Top with the green onions. Serve with a poached egg on the side.

6

FRUIT FOR BREAKFAST

It almost seems unnecessary to offer recipes for serving fruit at breakfast. Enjoyed fresh, just as it is, fruit is one of the simplest and purest breakfast foods.

Breakfast by the Seasons

For those of us without direct access to a kitchen garden or fruit tree, the opportunity to begin the day with a wide variety of fresh fruit is probably greater than it has been for generations.

Americans have long enjoyed an enviable bounty of fresh fruits and vegetables, thanks mainly to the modern supermarket. Our proximity to the temperate latitudes of the southern United States and Central and South America have helped to make tropical and semitropical treats such as bananas and citrus fruit especially popular at the morning meal.

Recently, Americans have begun to seek out a greater variety of produce, especially fruits and vegetables grown and processed without the chemicals needed to make them picture-perfect and durable. As a result, farmers' markets have sprung up throughout the country, in small towns and large cities alike. Such markets often feature organic produce as well as old-fashioned and uniquely local varieties too fragile or short-lived to suit the supermarket trade.

Shop regularly at the local farmers' market (or natural food store, which often offers a similar selection), and soon you'll begin to notice the seasons passing in a different way: strawberry season gives way to cherry season, followed by the seasons for apricots, peaches, melons, grapes, and so on.

Buying Seasonal Fruit

Here are the peak seasons for common fruit varieties, with some tips on what to look for. Growing seasons will differ with the region and the specific fruit variety.

"O precious food! Delight of the mouth! O, much better than gold, masterpiece of Apollo! O flower of all the fruits! O ravishing melon!"

—Marc Antoine de Gérard Saint-Amant

Season	Fruit	What to Look For
January to February	Tangerines	Brightly colored skin without soft or dark spots.
January to November	Valencia oranges	Thin, bright golden peel (some green is OK). Firm, heavy for its size, no soft or moldy spots.
April to July	Strawberries	Brightly colored, plump, green caps still attached, not bruised, shriveled, or moldy.

(continues)

91

Season	Fruit	What to Look For
May to June	Cherries	Brightly colored, shiny, plump. Sweet cherries (Bing and Royal Ann varieties) should be firm but not hard. Sour cherries (Montmorency and Morello varieties) should be medium-firm.
June to July	Apricots	Plump, reasonably firm, uniform color.
June to August	Watermelon	Dull (not shiny) rind that just barely yields to pressure. Hollow thump when slapped. For cut melons, look for brightly colored flesh, not grainy or dry-looking, without white seeds (indicates immature melon).
June to September	Cantaloupe	Heavy for its size, sweet, fruity fragrance, thick, well-raised netting on grayish-beige skin, yields to slight pressure on the blossom end. No soft spots or overly strong odor or seeds heard sloshing inside.

According to the *Guinness Book of World Records*, the world's largest cantaloupe was 62 pounds, raised by C. Draughtridge of Rocky Mount, North Carolina, in 1991.

Season	Fruit	What to Look For
June to September	Peaches	Intensely fragrant, gives slightly to palm pressure. Avoid those with greenish skin, soft spots.
June to October	Grapes	Plump, full-colored, firmly attached to stems. White green grapes (such as Thompson seedless and Ribier varieties) will be slightly pale yellow. Dark grapes (such as Red Flame and Tokay) will be deeply colored, without any sign of green.
July to September	Honeydew melons	Very heavy for its size, creamy yellow rind with almost imperceptible wrinkles.
July to October	Pears	Fragrant, no blemishes or soft spots. Asian, Bartlett, and Seckel are common summer and fall varieties.

To identify a vine-ripened melon, look for a clean break between the rind and the stem. If a bit of cut stem remains attached, the melon was probably harvested prematurely.

(continues)

93

Season	Fruit	What to Look For
September to April	Apples	Firm, well-colored, fresh (not musty) fragrance. Smooth skin with no bruises or gouges. Fuji, Granny Smith, Jonathan, and Red Delicious are common eating varieties. Gravenstein and Rome Beauty are well-suited to cooking.
October to April	Winter pears	Fragrant, no blemishes or soft spots. Colors and textures vary depending on the variety. Anjou, Bosc, and Comice are winter varieties.
December to May	Grapefruit	Heavy for its size, thin, finely textured, brightly colored skin, firm yet springy when squeezed.
December to May	Navel oranges	Thick, bright orange skin without wrinkles, soft or dark spots.

Fruit As Healthful Food

What more can be said about the benefits of a diet rich in fresh fruit? Ideally, fruit and other produce constitute a significant part of our daily diet, yet Americans still only eat about half of what they should.

Breakfast gives us the perfect opportunity to eat more fruit, which has long been a natural and familiar part of the meal. Single pieces of fruit, such as a banana, peach, or apple, make a quick meal-on-the-run requiring virtually no preparation. Bananas and dried fruit typically garnish our cereal or yogurt, while berries find their way into pancakes, waffles, and other baked goods. Fresh fruit salads and cooked fruit such as applesauce are typical breakfast side dishes. A grapefruit often constitutes an entire breakfast, as does melon, of which there are many varieties available throughout the summer months.

Combining fresh fruit is like painting with a palette of flavors, colors, and textures. The goal should be a simple, pleasing harmony, with the best qualities of each ingredient given the chance to shine. Cooking fruit helps to intensify and blend flavors. It also helps to soften hard fruits or redeem fruit that has an uninteresting texture when raw. Cooked fruit

often serves to complement or contrast foods with rich or assertive flavors.

Minted Three-Melon Salad

This salad makes a healthy, quick meal when served with a bran muffin and fresh juice. The lime juice and mint help to enliven a less-than-completely flavorful melon.

SERVES 4 TO 6

$^1/_2$ each of three different firm-fleshed melons (such as
    cantaloupe, honeydew, and Crenshaw), peeled and seeded
$^1/_2$ cup (firmly packed) fresh mint, finely chopped
Juice of 3 limes

Cut the melon flesh into 1-inch cubes (or use a medium to large melon baller). Place in a large nonreactive mixing bowl and toss gently and thoroughly with the mint and lime juice (add more lime juice if desired). Transfer to a glass serving bowl, cover, and chill for at least 1 hour before serving.

Ambrosia

This is actually a classic side dish served at holiday dinners in the South—Jim's mother remembers it from childhood Christmas dinners in Florida—but the flavors and colors make it ideal for breakfast. Common variations call for adding bananas, grapes, pineapple, and other fruit, but we think this most traditional version is the simplest and best.

SERVES 4 TO 6

"If I could have cherries when it is freezing and amber-colored melon in the heart of winter, what pleasure would I take in them when my palate needs neither moistening or cooling?"

–Jean-Jacques Rousseau

6 large seedless oranges
2 cups packaged shredded coconut (or grated fresh coconut)
2 to 3 tablespoons powdered sugar

Cut the rinds and whitish membranes from the oranges.
Thinly slice the oranges crosswise. Make one layer of overlapping orange slices in a glass serving dish, sprinkle with some
of the coconut, and dust with some of the powdered sugar.
Repeat for several more layers (the number depends on
the size and depth of the dish), ending with the coconut and
another light dusting of powdered sugar. Cover and refrigerate
for at least one hour before serving.

A perfectly ripe pineapple will have a small, compact crown of leaves and make a solid, hollow sound when thumped. The color of the skin or flesh is not an indicator of ripeness.

Broiled Grapefruit

This rather old-fashioned preparation gives grapefruit a darker, more complex flavor. It's easy to prepare at the last minute for brunch.

SERVES 2

1 grapefruit, halved
1 tablespoon brown sugar, or more to taste

Preheat the broiler. Section the flesh in each grapefruit half
using a grapefruit or paring knife. Sprinkle each half with
brown sugar. Place each half cut side up on a baking sheet
and run under the broiler until the sugar begins to caramelize.
Serve warm.

Fresh Citrus Compote

This is an elegant and colorful addition to brunch. The honey adds just the lightest note of sweetness. Use this recipe as a springboard for combining other fruits.

SERVES 6 TO 8

2 pink grapefruit
2 navel oranges
2 blood oranges (or 3 tangerines)
1 pineapple
²/₃ cup orange juice
¹/₂ cup honey
¹/₂ cup Madeira (optional)

Cut away the rind and membranes of the grapefruit and oranges. Slice the grapefruit into sections. Slice the oranges crosswise. Peel, core, and slice the pineapple and cut into 1-inch pieces. Place all the fruit in a clear glass bowl.

In a small nonreactive saucepan, bring the orange juice, honey, and Madeira to a boil for 1 minute. Allow to cool to room temperature. Pour over the fruit and toss right before serving.

Peaches and Cream

Much as we'd like to, we really can't take credit for this preparation. We offer it simply as one of the best ways to eat a perfect peach. The skin is essential to the experience—remove any excess fuzz by gently rubbing the peach in a clean dish towel. This is also an excellent way to enjoy a single, perfectly ripe banana or a basket of fresh berries.

SERVES 1

1 peach (preferably a freestone variety)
Cold milk or half-and-half to taste

With a paring knife, cut the peach in quarters, gently twist it open, and remove the pit. Cut each quarter into several slices or chunks and place in a bowl. Pour the milk or cream over the fruit.

Fried Apples

This is another Southern classic that adds a delicious sweetness when accompanying eggs, bacon, or sausage. Don't shy away from the small amount of bacon fat used in this recipe—it adds an irreplaceable savory flavor (with a nonstick skillet, you don't need much).

SERVES 6 TO 8

6 to 8 firm tart green apples (such as Granny Smith)
2 tablespoons bacon fat
White or brown sugar to taste

Core and slice the apples, leaving the skin on. In a 10- to 12-inch nonstick skillet, heat the bacon fat over medium heat and add the apples. Cook uncovered, turning frequently and adding sugar to taste, until the apples are golden and tender but still hold their shape. Serve hot.

Applesauce

This recipe captures the flavors of apple pie, but in much less time.

MAKES 2 1/2 CUPS

5 large cooking apples (such as Gravenstein or Rome Beauty),
    peeled, cored, and quartered
1/2 cup apple juice
Juice of two lemons
1/4 cup plus 2 tablespoons brown sugar
1/2 teaspoon ground cinnamon
1/4 teaspoon ground ginger

Cut the quartered apples into several pieces. Combine with the remaining ingredients in a heavy, nonreactive 3-quart saucepan. Bring to a boil, then reduce the heat and simmer uncovered over medium-low heat for about 30 minutes, stirring frequently to prevent scorching. Add a little more apple juice if more liquid is needed. As the apples soften, break them up with a mixing spoon and mash them against the sides of the pan. After about 30 minutes, the sauce will be a coarse, golden puree with a small amount of liquid. Serve warm or cover and refrigerate for several days.

7

BREAKFAST DRINKS AND BEVERAGES

For many of us, waking up is a feat in itself. To engage our brains and awaken our appetites, we often turn to a cup of hot coffee or a glass of cold juice.

A Tradition of Stimulating Beverages

For obvious reasons, stimulating beverages have long been standard morning fare. Up through the 1700s, beer was the preferred morning stimulant in Europe. Tea, consumed in Asia for at least several millennia, reached Europe in the seventeenth century and replaced beer at the breakfast table in eighteenth century Germany. But no sooner had it reached the New World than colonial Americans staged the Boston Tea Party in 1773, the event that made coffee a permanent part of the American breakfast.

The basics for making coffee have changed remarkably little since a drink from dried coffee beans was first made in the tenth-century Middle East (before that time, coffee beans were eaten raw or fermented for wine). Originally, coffee beans were ground to a powder, then infused with boiling water to make a thick drink, a process that resembles the modern American method for making "cowboy coffee."

In the nineteenth century, woven and perforated metal screens and, later, paper filters were used to remove the grit.

The percolator, invented in 1825, combines boiling and infusing into one operation. Espresso machines perform the brewing process by forcing pressurized steam through finely ground beans. More and more homes rely on automatic drip coffeemakers. Some include timers, so their owners can quite literally wake up and smell the coffee (we know people who use theirs as olfactory alarm clocks). The most sophisticated models both grind and brew.

A Perfect Cup of Coffee

✦ Use good-quality coffee beans, ideally from a local roaster, who can tell you about different bean varieties and roasts. Store the beans in an airtight container, as prolonged exposure to air turns coffee stale and rancid.

✦ Grind the beans just before brewing. Use about two tablespoons of grounds for every six ounces of water, using more or less depending on the type of bean, the brewing method, and the desired strength.

✦ Start with cold water, freshly drawn (filtered or purified is better). Brew with water just off the boil to release the best flavor compounds. Avoid boiling the water while brewing, as occurs with a percolator (a method we're reluctant to

Caffeine per 6-ounce cup	
Espresso (2 ounces)	60 to 90 mg
Drip coffee	60 to 180 mg
Black tea	25 to 110 mg
Oolong tea	12 to 55 mg
Green tea	8 to 16 mg

103

recommend), which hastens the breakdown of flavor molecules into sour-tasting acids.

✦ Try making drip or filtered coffee. Paper filters trap bitter-tasting oils and produce an exceptionally clear, smooth cup of coffee. Unbleached paper filters are said to leach out chemicals suspected of raising blood cholesterol levels. Gold mesh filters produce a good flavorful brew with none of the paper waste.

✦ Drink freshly brewed coffee right away. If you must hold it longer, keep it in an insulated carafe or thermos—coffee left on the coffeemaker burner loses desirable flavor components and soon tastes burnt. Reheating leftover coffee probably isn't worth the effort.

Yule Latte

The popularity of home espresso machines makes it possible to enjoy cafe-style drinks anytime. This wintertime treat is from A Cozy Book of Coffees & Cocoas.

SERVES 2

2 shots espresso
1 1/2 cups eggnog
2 tablespoons powdered white chocolate
2 teaspoons hazelnut syrup

Ground cinnamon
Freshly grated nutmeg

Brew the espresso and briefly set it aside. Place the eggnog in a cold frothing pitcher and steam. Since eggnog is so rich, you will not get a lot of froth, but some will develop as you heat it through. Place 1 tablespoon white chocolate and 1 teaspoon hazelnut syrup in the bottom of each warm mug and pour in equal amounts of steamed eggnog. Stir to dissolve the chocolate and syrup. Place a long-handled spoon in each warm mug, then cap off with a bit of froth. Pour a shot of espresso down the center of each mug. Dust with cinnamon and nutmeg and serve immediately.

Cafe au Lait

Sip a cup while nibbling a croissant and dream of breakfast in Paris.
SERVES 2

1 cup each brewed, dark-roasted coffee (such as French or
Italian Roast) and milk

Brew a pot of strong coffee using the drip or filter method. Meanwhile, place the milk in a small saucepan and heat over medium until very hot but not boiling. Pour the hot milk into a pitcher. When the coffee is ready, pour equal parts hot milk and hot coffee into two or more mugs. Serve immediately.

"Trim over last year's hat, if you must, and buy no books for a year except this one, but do have the daily coffee right."

–Olive Green, *What to Have for Breakfast* (1905)

Brewed Coffee with Cinnamon and Nutmeg

This aromatic brew from A Cozy Book of Coffees & Cocoas *features classic Mexican flavors.*

<small>SERVES</small> **4**

$1/2$ cup ground medium-bodied coffee
$1/4$ teaspoon ground cinnamon
$1/8$ teaspoon (scant) freshly ground nutmeg
3 cups cold water

Place the coffee grounds in a filter basket and sprinkle the cinnamon and nutmeg on top. Brew the coffee by drip or filter method. Serve immediately in warm cups.

A Soothing Pot of Tea

Tea is the alternative for those of us who want a warm lift in the morning but don't necessarily need to start the day with a bang.

A single species of plant produces all varieties of tea, although the characteristics of the end product vary considerably with the country of origin and the processing method. There are two main types of tea: black tea and green tea. For black tea, freshly harvested tea leaves are fermented before being dried, while green tea is produced by drying the leaves immediately (Oolong tea, produced from semifermented leaves, is unique). Herbal teas aren't really teas at all but fresh and dried herbs and other fragrant and flavorful plant materials.

Here are some familiar varieties of tea:

Darjeeling	Grown in northern India. Noted for its complexity, clarity, and flavorful lightness.
Earl Grey	Chinese black or Darjeeling tea scented with oil of bergamot, derived from a Mediterranean citrus fruit.
English Breakfast	A blend of black teas from Ceylon, India, and China. With a medium body and brisk flavor, it is usually drunk with milk.
Irish Breakfast	More complex, pungent, and substantial than English Breakfast.
Jasmine	Green tea that was dried next to fresh jasmine blossoms, which lend a floral scent and flavor.
Keemun	The most celebrated Chinese black tea. Sweet, somewhat smoky, with the fragrance of roses or orchids.
Lapsang Suchong	A Chinese black tea smoked over pine wood fires. Dark, pungent, and unusual.

The act of brewing tea is its own little ritual within the larger ritual of preparing breakfast. Setting out the teapot and cups, putting the kettle on to boil, and measuring, steeping, and pouring the tea—whether performed in the traditional Japanese manner or in a warm kitchen on a blustery winter morning, these steps create a pleasing, purposeful harmony.

✦ Allow one teaspoon of tea leaves for each 5 to 6 ounces of boiling water. Loose tea allows for the fullest infusion, since the tea leaves can unfurl completely, although a loosely packed tea ball simplifies the cleanup. For herbal teas, one rule of thumb is to allow $1/2$ to 1 tablespoon of fresh material or $1/4$ to $1/2$ teaspoon of dried material per cup of water, but experiment with amounts to suit your own taste.

✦ Start with cold, freshly drawn water. Use just off the boil.

✦ Just before adding the tea leaves and water, warm the teapot by rinsing it once or twice with boiling water.

✦ Let the tea steep for 3 to 5 minutes, then strain it promptly. Herbal teas may require longer infusion times.

✦ Listen to the British: they'll tell you milk is best suited to the subtle flavors of tea (cream has too much fat).

"A great deal too much against tea is said by wise people, and a great deal too much of tea is given to the sick by foolish people."

—Florence Nightingale

✧ Use a ceramic or enamel teapot. Some purists advise against metal teapots, ignoring the traditional Japanese cast-iron teapot, but in any case, avoid aluminum, which reacts with the acids in tea and creates an unpleasant metallic flavor.

Chocolate

Nowhere does the distinction between breakfast and dessert grow blurrier than when it comes to chocolate. We're reluctant to call this a breakfast food—it's really more of a treat (notwithstanding its increasing and rather questionable presence in such morning foods as packaged dry cereals and muffins). Still, we fondly recall our own anticipation at being allowed to have chocolate milk with breakfast. Who are we to deny others this pleasure?

Mexican Hot Chocolate

A mug of this delicious chocolate and a Cream and Cranberry Scone (page 71) make a welcoming, warming wintertime treat.

SERVES 6 TO 8

4 cups whole or low-fat milk
1/2 cup brown sugar
1 teaspoon ground cinnamon
2 teaspoons vanilla extract
4 ounces unsweetened chocolate, chopped

In a medium saucepan, bring the milk, brown sugar, cinnamon, and vanilla to a boil. Remove from the heat immediately, add the chocolate, and stir until smooth. Return the mixture to medium-high heat, bring to a simmer, then whisk constantly for 2 minutes. Remove from the heat and serve in heavy mugs.

Juices

There's a reason orange juice is called "liquid sunshine." The bright color and flavor of a freshly squeezed glassful have the same effect as throwing open the blinds on a sunny morning.

The sparkle and color of juices awaken the eye just as the flavor awakens the tongue. Drinking juice is the easiest way to consume the day's recommended amount of fruits and vegetables. By far the most familiar homemade juice (also the most easily made at home) comes from oranges. Valencia oranges are the sweetest variety, prized for juicing. Juice from the other citrus fruits is definitely worth the small amount of extra effort. To those who only know orange juice, freshly squeezed tangerine juice, for example, will be a revelation—bright, intense, and equally sweet and tart.

Beware of commercially produced juices said to be "freshly squeezed" or "not made from concentrate"—they're seldom more than poor substitutes for truly fresh juice made in your own kitchen. Home juicers, though pricey, make it possible to produce the freshest and most healthful juices from many other types of produce.

Watermelon Juice

Never thought about juice from a melon? Actually, this juice recalls aquas frescas, *the refreshing Mexican fruit drinks, of which watermelon is just one of many varieties. The amount of juice you'll produce for this recipe depends on the size of the melon and the moistness of the flesh. Use the sweetest melon you can find.*

SERVES 3 TO 4

Half of a large watermelon (about 7 to 8 pounds total), chilled
    if possible
2 to 3 tablespoons superfine sugar (optional)

Using a large spoon, remove the watermelon flesh from the rind and place in a large stainless steel or glass bowl (don't worry about the seeds). Working in several batches, transfer the flesh to a blender jar or food processor work bowl fitted with a steel blade. Pulse briefly and repeatedly to break up the flesh (this will occur almost immediately) but not so much as to grind the seeds. Pour the puree through a medium-fine strainer, pressing any remaining chunks with the back of a large spoon to extract the juice. Taste for sweetness and add sugar as needed. Serve chilled.

Ginger Lover's Cocktail

This nonalcoholic cocktail just screams to be served in a tall glass with a paper umbrella. Ideal for a summertime brunch crowd, it supplies that warm, gingery glow. The quantities below can easily be reduced by half.

SERVES 16

8 cups pineapple juice
1/3 pound fresh ginger, peeled and chopped coarsely
1 cup lemon juice
1 1/2 cups sugar
crushed ice

In a large nonreactive bowl, mix the pineapple juice with 6 cups of water. In a blender, puree the ginger with 2 cups of water. Spread a clean dish towel on the counter or a flat surface. Place the puree in the center, gather up the corners of the towel and wring as much juice as possible from the puree into the bowl containing the pineapple juice. Add the lemon juice and sugar to taste. Chill thoroughly and serve over crushed ice.

Fruit Smoothies

Smoothies combine all the best features of breakfast in one utopian preparation. Like the best breakfast treats, they're sweet, thick, and creamy (think "breakfast milkshake"). They brim with vitamins and fiber and are easily made with virtually no fat. They're the perfect vehicle for individual expression and improvisation and, best of all, they're fast. So forget all those excuses for skipping breakfast—a smoothie and a muffin (baked the night before to save time, of course) make the ideal last-minute breakfast-on-the-run. Here are the basic elements:

❖ Unsweetened citrus juices and fruit nectars work especially well.

❖ Yogurt or milk. Besides adding protein, yogurt lends creaminess. Flavored and frozen yogurt offer interesting possibilities. Use a little milk to adjust the consistency.

❖ Fruit, preferably fresh (frozen and canned varieties also work well). Especially good are fleshy fruits, like peaches and melons, berries of all kinds, and tropical fruits such as bananas and pineapple. When frozen and used straight from the freezer, bananas contribute a remarkable creaminess as well as the necessary chill (ice won't be necessary).

❖ Flavorings such as grated fresh ginger, freshly squeezed lemon or lime juice, coconut meat (freshly grated or packaged), or canned coconut milk, which is available in Asian markets and specialty groceries, and fresh herbs, such as mint or even basil.

Apricot Smoothie

SERVES 2

2 cups apricot nectar
1/4 cup nonfat plain yogurt
1 frozen banana, peeled
2 teaspoons finely grated fresh ginger

Place all the ingredients in a blender jar and blend until smooth and frothy. Serve immediately.

Orange-Banana Smoothie

SERVES 2

2 cups orange juice
1/4 cup nonfat plain yogurt
1 frozen banana, peeled

Place all the ingredients in a blender jar and blend until smooth and frothy. Serve immediately.

Pineapple-Coconut Smoothie

SERVES 2

2 cups pineapple juice
1/4 cup nonfat plain yogurt
2 tablespoons coconut milk (found at Asian markets and specialty groceries)

Twelve percent of all cola soft drinks sold are consumed with (or in place of) breakfast.

¹/₂ cup fresh or canned pineapple chunks
¹/₂ fresh or frozen banana, peeled
1 tablespoon finely grated fresh ginger

Place all the ingredients in a blender jar and blend until smooth and frothy. Serve immediately.

Morning Cocktails

One of the stricter rules about the morning meal concerns the prohibition against drinking or serving alcoholic beverages before noon. Perhaps this rule reflects health-conscious sensibilities or the childlike nature of the meal itself, with its many sweet and creamy temptations. However, like most other rules about breakfast, there's always an exception when it comes to brunch, when we welcome the sense of adult indulgence and festivity that certain alcoholic concoctions bring to the occasion.

Kir Royale

Champagne is the one wine deemed appropriate for any food, and breakfast foods should be no exception. Champagne lightens rich flavors and textures and lends a note of festive sophistication. The crème de cassis gives this classic French aperitif a delicate, rosy hue and berry-like perfume. When made with dry white wine in place of champagne, this drink is known simply as Kir.

SERVES 6

1 (750-ml) bottle of good-quality dry champagne or sparkling wine, well chilled
3 to 4 teaspoons crème de cassis

Place 1/2 teaspoon of crème de cassis in each of six champagne flutes. Fill the glass with champagne and serve immediately.

Mimosa

An elegant brunch classic, especially refreshing in summertime.

SERVES 8

2 cups orange juice (preferably freshly squeezed)
1/2 cup Grand Marnier or other orange-flavored liqueur
2 (750 ml) bottles of extra-dry champagne or sparkling wine

Mix the orange juice and orange liqueur. Divide among eight champagne glasses. Slowly add the wine to fill. Serve immediately.

Ramos Gin Fizz

This is the original gin fizz, a New Orleans classic, and it's perfect for a springtime brunch. With all the egg whites it calls for, it's a perfect partner for Eggs Benedict (see 13).

SERVES 6 TO 8

1 cup gin
2 tablespoons half-and-half
$^1/_2$ cup superfine sugar
2 cups crushed ice
1 $^1/_2$ teaspoons orange flower water
$^3/_4$ cup fresh lemon juice
6 egg whites

Combine all the ingredients in a blender. Blend on high until frothy. Serve immediately.

It's estimated that half of all the coffee consumed in America is consumed at breakfast time.

"Water is the only drink for a wise man."

—Henry David Thoreau

8

BRUNCH (OR BREAKFAST WITHOUT RULES)

If breakfast is personal, then brunch is social. Like the word it-self—a portmanteau term borrowed from English university slang that combines "breakfast" and "lunch"—the meal is a casual affair with no particular rules. Brunch is what you make it.

At home, brunch can be as simple as a basket of muffins and a pitcher of juice shared with friends after a Saturday morning game of tennis—it's the company that matters. At the other extreme is the Sunday brunch served at San Francisco's Sheraton Palace Hotel in the Garden Court, the hotel's sumptuous, skylit Victorian-era dining room. Guests serve themselves from a dozen buffets that feature everything from pancakes, waffles, French toast, and eggs made to order to fresh seafood, cold vegetable salads, pasta, prime rib, and every imaginable type of pastry. Freshly squeezed orange juice and champagne flow nonstop. But the food wouldn't be half as memorable if it weren't for the grand setting, the company, and the sheer occasion of it all.

An American Meal

Americans were enjoying brunch long before there was a word for it. American pundit H. L. Mencken reportedly introduced the term on this side of the Atlantic in a 1900 newspaper account of the social fad then sweeping London. By that time, residents of New Orleans had been eating virtually the same meal for at least twenty years.

In 1880, New Orleans restaurateur Elizabeth Kettenring Dutrey Begué introduced "second breakfast" at her French Quarter establishment. She served this lavish buffet for shop-keepers, bakers, produce merchants, and butchers at 11 A.M. each morning after the initial rush of shoppers in the quarter's open-air market. The meal was a New Orleans institution when Madame Begué died in 1906 and was continued by her husband for another eleven years.

What to Eat for Brunch

There are really no brunch foods per se. Rather, brunch features standard breakfast fare embellished with special-occasion ingredients and a social purpose.

Certain foods, such as hot or cold cereal, may seem too mundane for brunch, although not necessarily in a weekend ski cabin, for example. Other foods not typically served in the morning, such as fish or chocolate, can lend the meal a sense of occasion. The lighter dishes once associated with teas and ladies' luncheons—crepes, quiche, and light casseroles—are now thought of as standard brunch fare. Brunch is also something of a grown-up's meal, this being one of the only

occasions before noon when one may properly serve alcoholic drinks.

Turning Breakfast into Brunch

✦ Invite friends, family, or neighbors to share the meal. Host a brunch in honor of visiting out-of-town guests.

✦ Break out the good dishes, flatware, and table linens. Decorate the table with a vase of freshly cut flowers.

✦ Put on favorite music, something suited to the occasion but unobtrusive.

✦ Serve the meal buffet-style and arrange seating to promote conversation.

✦ Make preparation of the meal part of the occasion. Invite your guests into the kitchen to help with specific tasks, such as brewing coffee, making toast, or setting the table.

✦ Serve the meal outdoors on the patio or in the garden under a shady tree.

✦ Plan the meal to precede another social activity such as an afternoon around the swimming pool, a leisurely bike ride, or playtime for small children.

Brunch Menus

Any breakfast can become brunch, limited only by the extent of one's imagination. Here are just a few suggestions for brunches throughout the year.

A Quick, Healthy Brunch

This menu is easily assembled for a casual get-together after a Saturday morning workout or a brisk walk in the park. Make the muffins ahead and store them tightly wrapped until served. Have the coffee ready to brew before you leave the house. Plan to make the smoothies to order.

- ✧ Bran Muffins (page 65)
- ✧ Fruit Smoothies (page 112)
- ✧ Coffee or tea

A Light Brunch

This menu is perfect for after church or whenever a morning guest drops by unexpectedly. The Raspberry Coffee Cake should be served the day you make it, but the Sour Cream Coffee Cake will keep for a day or two.

- ✦ Raspberry Coffee Cake (page 72) or Sour Cream Coffee Cake (page 74)

- ✦ Fresh fruit

- ✦ Coffee or tea

Cinco de Mayo Brunch

May 5th is the anniversary of Mexico's independence from France. The celebration is marked with dancing, singing, and fireworks. This menu glows with equally vibrant Mexican flavors: chilies, orange, coconut, cinnamon, and nutmeg. If the days have turned warm by early May, brew the coffee on the strong side and serve it iced.

- ✦ Chili Relleno Casserole (page 21)

- ✦ Ambrosia (page 96)

- ✦ Brewed Coffee with Cinnamon and Nutmeg (page 106)

An Elegant Brunch

Poached eggs and mimosas really dress up this menu. The ingredients for the potatoes can be prepared the night before for assembly at the last minute. Even the eggs can be prepared before guests arrive and held for reheating right before serving.

✦ Poached Eggs (page 12)

✦ Brunch Potatoes (page 86)

✦ Mimosa (page 116)

✦ Coffee or tea

Holiday Brunch

When the demands of the winter holidays pile up, holiday socializing is often the first to go. This menu makes it possible to entertain with a minimum of last-minute activity. Only the green salad needs any real attention before serving time (given the rich flavors of the Union Square Brunch, be sure to keep the salad simple).

✦ Union Square Brunch (page 26)

✦ Green salad

✦ Champagne or sparking wine

✦ Yule Latte (page 104)

Dressy Springtime Brunch

Plan to serve this menu when you have plenty of time to relax and visit. Serving Eggs Benedict with Hollandaise Sauce, which calls for extra egg yolks, provides the perfect excuse for making Ramos Gin Fizzes, which require egg whites. The clean, sharp flavors of the Fresh Citrus Compote contrast nicely with the richness of the rest of the menu.

- ❖ Eggs Benedict (page 13)
- ❖ Fresh Citrus Compote (page 98)
- ❖ Ramos Gin Fizz (page 116)
- ❖ Coffee or tea

Weekend Getaway Brunch

Kitchens in weekend houses can be unpredictable, but that doesn't mean an out-of-town brunch can't be special. Even if you can only count on a stove and a skillet, you're still equipped to surprise your guests with this simple but stylish and flavorful menu. Make the crepes and sausage ahead of time—even the filling can be made ahead. The final assembly is so simple, the chef can sleep in, too!

- Crepes with Pear Filling (page 55)

- Sweet Italian Chicken Sausage (page 82)

- Coffee, tea, or juice

A Birthday Brunch

Let the extravagantly puffed German Oven Pancake stand in for a birthday cake—when it's served hot from the oven, the presentation will be just as memorable. If you can't do without a cake, this menu is light enough to ensure that your guests will still have room.

- German Oven Pancake (page 52)

- Minted Three-Melon Salad (page 96)

- Champagne

- Coffee, tea, or juice

Index

NOTES

NOTES

International Conversion Chart

These are not exact equivalents: they have been slightly rounded to make measuring easier.

LIQUID MEASUREMENTS

American	Imperial	Metric	Australian
2 tablespoons (1 oz.)	1 fl. oz.	30 ml	1 tablespoon
1/4 cup (2 oz.)	2 fl. oz.	60 ml	2 tablespoons
1/3 cup (3 oz.)	3 fl. oz.	80 ml	1/4 cup
1/2 cup (4 oz.)	4 fl. oz.	125 ml	1/3 cup
2/3 cup (5 oz.)	5 fl. oz.	165 ml	1/2 cup
3/4 cup (6 oz.)	6 fl. oz.	185 ml	2/3 cup
1 cup (8 oz.)	8 fl. oz.	250 ml	3/4 cup

SPOON MEASUREMENTS

American	Metric
1/4 teaspoon	1 ml
1/2 teaspoon	2 ml
1 teaspoon	5 ml
1 tablespoon	15 ml

WEIGHTS

US/UK	Metric
1 oz.	30 grams (g)
2 oz.	60 g
4 oz. (1/4 lb)	125 g
5 oz. (1/3 lb)	155 g
6 oz.	185 g
7 oz.	220 g
8 oz. (1/2 lb)	250 g
10 oz.	315 g
12 oz. (3/4 lb)	375 g
14 oz.	440 g
16 oz. (1 lb)	500 g
2 lbs	1 kg

OVEN TEMPERATURES

Farenheit	Centigrade	Gas
250	120	1/2
300	150	2
325	160	3
350	180	4
375	190	5
400	200	6
450	230	8